Papercrafting
room by room

30 one-of-a-kind accents for your home

Deborah Spofford

North Light Books
Cincinnati, Ohio
www.artistsnetwork.com

about the author

Deborah Spofford has been a professional craft designer since 1996, writing articles for craft magazines, creating sewing pattern booklets and authoring craft booklets for Plaid, Hot Off the Press, Leisure Arts and House of White Birches. Her work has appeared in Craftworks, Country Marketplace, Crafts magazine, Crafts n' Things and Country Crafts. In addition to her published works, Deborah works with several manufacturers to find creative ways to use and promote their products. She also shares her craft and decorating ideas monthly on AM Northwest, a regional television program, and has appeared on the Carol Duvall Show. Deborah lives in Vancouver, Washington, with her husband Tim, and their children Tucker and Abbey.

09 08 07 06 05   5 4 3 2 1

Library of Congress Cataloging-in-Publication Data

Spofford, Deborah
      Papercrafting room by room: 30 one-of-a-kind accents for your home / Deborah Spofford.--1st ed.
              p. cm.
      Includes index
      ISBN 1-58180-656-6 (alk. paper)
       1. Paper work. 2. House furnishings. 3. Interior decoration. I. Title

      TT870.S673 2005
      745.54--dc22

                              2004059528

Editor: Tonia Davenport

Cover Designer: Karla Baker

Interior Designer: Leigh Ann Lentz

Layout Artist: Jessica Schultz

Production Coordinator: Robin Richie

Photographers: Hal Barkan, Tim Grondin and Christine Polomsky

Stylist: Jan Nickum

F+W PUBLICATIONS, INC.

dedication

To the joys of my life, my husband of 25 years, Tim, and my children, Tucker and Abbey. Also to our daughter Timborah who touched our lives for only a short time but continues to bless us every day with her spirit.

acknowledgments

Thanks to my editor, Tonia Davenport (a previous Washingtonian), for her guidance, wisdom and organization and to Tricia Waddell at F+W Publications for believing in and promoting my book idea!

I would also like to thank Lori Maritato at Graphic Products Corporation for helping me procure the beautiful papers used in this book and for pointing me in the right direction to the company Web site, www.gpcpapers.com, which provided an enormous amount of information about Black Ink papers from around the world.

Our family has been blessed in so many ways and through the joys and the heartaches, the gift of creativity has always been a comfort and a delight. The opportunity to write this book is one of God's wonderful blessings.

table of contents

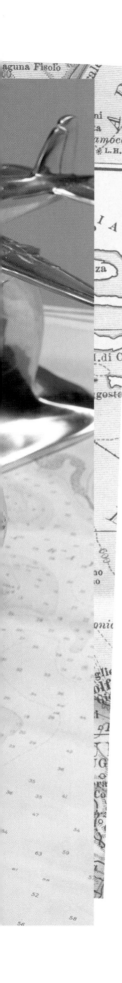

introduction

What can I tell you? I have fallen in love with paper.

The ideas for the projects in this book came about because I am absolutely, incredibly inspired by the decorative papers that are currently on the market for scrapbooking, card making and rubber stamping. I could easily become a paperaholic and fill my studio with different colors and textures of papers.

Although I regularly design papercraft projects as a part of my profession, home décor is my first love. That was the inspiration for this book. I wanted to take beautiful papers and find a way to use them for home decorating. This book is filled with projects that do just that. You'll find elegant papers used to transform generic items such as lamp-shades, vases and furniture into sophisticated accessories for your home. You will learn how to add dimension (literally and figuratively) to paper projects that will freshen up your living spaces.

The projects on the following pages look sophisticated, but believe me, they are incredibly easy to make. I love to inspire and help self-proclaimed "non-crafters" discover they really can do it! Whether you are a beginning crafter or an expert, you will find projects in this book that will fuel your creativity.

The foundation surfaces for all of the projects can be found in mass merchandise stores and the rest of the materials you may already have in your craft room! Handmade papers are readily available so you can skip the messy step of making your own papers and jump right to the fun part. You will revisit some old techniques and learn a few new ones. You will also find suggestions about how to use the projects in your home and for gift giving. Are you ready?

Paper!

You cannot imagine my excitement when I found the papers that are used in this book. My proposal for the book had already been accepted when I began my search for the "perfect papers." There are many decorative papers on the market for scrapbooking, but I was looking for something different. I wanted unique papers that were large enough to make home décor projects.

I found the papers while I was attending a trade show in Dallas, Texas. This particular show is very large and after walking around for a while you feel like you have spent the day on a high-speed treadmill. I was disappointed because I could not find what I was looking for. My flight was later that evening, but I was tempted to leave early and start packing for the trip home. All the papers that I had seen that day were the same old thing with a few variations. I decided to walk down one more aisle and then I would make my escape and head back to the hotel. I got about halfway down that aisle when I saw them—the "perfect papers"! I was instantly inspired by the colors, designs, textures and patterns. And, they were available in large sheets! I stood in the booth for a while and started imagining the possibilities. I think I may have been drooling! I left the show knowing I had found what I was looking for.

I think you, too, will enjoy the selection of papers that are used. The sheets range in size from 25" × 37" to 20" × 30" (64cm × 94cm to 59cm × 76cm). Several of them are also available in 12" (30cm) squares. The papers are made by hand and by machine and come from many different countries. There are papers from Japan, India, the Philippines, Thailand, Korea and Nepal. Don't let that scare you though; they are all readily available through retail stores and the Internet.

Paper is made in different ways and from different materials.
Here is some information you may find interesting.

Batik

Batik is a technique that is used for fabric design. I had
no idea that it was also used for making paper. Wax is
dropped onto handmade paper before it is dyed. Wherever
the wax is, the dye cannot be absorbed. You can actually
feel the raised wax spots on the paper.

Woodblock

In this technique, a design is placed onto the base paper
with a wood block. Most of this is done by hand. Some
very beautiful patterns are created with this technique.

Layered

Different layers of paper are added to the base paper to
add design and color variations. The design is only seen
on one side of the paper.

Embossed

Embossed paper is made with a raised or depressed
design in the surface of the paper. The design can be
anything from wood grains to dragonflies.

Plants and Fibers Used in Paper

Paper is made from many different natural materials
which, in turn, come from many different countries. Here
are some of the ones you'll see in this book:

Mulberry: Japanese tree used for making paper.
Its leaves feed the silkworm.

Cotton: As the purest form of cellulose in nature,
this fiber requires little processing. It is also
known as rag or linters.

Kozo: Long, rough fibers from the mulberry
family.

Hemp: Manila hemp is related to the banana
plant, and its leaves are used to make paper.

Salago: A wild shrub native to the Philippines.

There are additional descriptions of the
papers throughout the book as they are used
in the individual projects.

Basic Materials

The basic materials used in this book are all fairly common and can be found in arts and crafts stores as well as specialty paper and rubber stamping stores.

Découpage Mediums

For the majority of the projects in this book, you will want to have the following découpage mediums on hand. They are all used to adhere paper to a surface, while at the same time, they act as a sealant to protect the paper.

Liquid Laminate

The laminate product that I use, Beacon's Liquid Laminate, is slightly thicker than water and is not sticky until it starts to dry. It works well with heavy handmade papers and lightweight papers like mulberry. The laminate actually soaks into the paper and becomes part of the paper's makeup when it is dry. It makes the paper pliable and in some cases molds pieces of paper back together after they have been torn.

Découpage Medium

This medium is much thicker than the laminate product and is very sticky. It looks milky when it is first applied, but dries perfectly clear. I like to use this with scrapbook papers that are less porous than handmade papers. Mod Podge is my découpage medium of choice because it does not soak instantly into the paper (with a few exceptions) but remains on the surface.

Paper Glaze

Paper glaze is a dimensional, varnish-like substance. It adds a thick glossy finish to paper. I used it several times to add a lacquer-like finish to the papers.

Paints & Stain

Acrylic paints can be combined with découpage mediums to tint your papers. They also can provide a base of color to your surface before any paper is applied.

Acrylic and Metal Paints

There are many different acrylic paints available. For one or two projects in this book you will need red and black. Look for the brands that are actually made for crafts versus artists' painting. To paint on metal, like the Retro Tray on page 52, look for metal paint. This paint is designed specifically to use on metal surfaces. I prefer Delta's No Primer Metal Colors.

Stain

I like the consistency of gel stain for wood projects. It is easier to control the color and it does not drip and run like other stains.

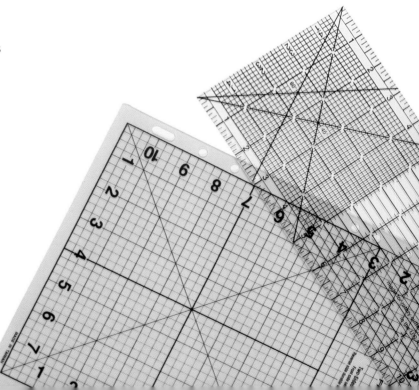

Tools

The tools needed to complete the projects in this book are minimal. You probably already have many of them at your disposal. Be sure and change the blades of your cutting tools often for the cleanest cuts.

Shape Cutter

I consider the ShapeCutter cutting system by Fiskars to be one of the most valuable tools that I have. It saves time and makes precise cuts that are difficult, if not impossible, to achieve with scissors. The ShapeCutter can be used two ways. It can be used with templates and it can be used for free style cutting. Both of these cutting methods require a different blade setting.

Rotary Cutter

The rotary cutter is a useful tool for cutting straight lines. It is a handheld cutter with a round, disc-shaped blade. It was originally designed for the quilting industry, but it is very useful for paper crafts as well. I like the Fiskars Softtouch rotary cutter because it has a comfortable handle and the blades are easy to change. It also has safety features not found on other cutters. In addition to the cutter, you will need a self-healing mat to protect your work surface and an acrylic ruler.

Acrylic Rulers

Acrylic rulers come in numerous sizes and shapes and are clear so you can see what you are cutting. They have measurement grids so it is easy to cut the size of paper that you want. I use either a 6" × 24" (15cm × 61cm) or a 6" × 12" (15cm × 30cm) ruler for most of my projects, but many other sizes would work just as well.

Cutting Mat

A cutting mat is an essential tool if you are working with a rotary cutter or the ShapeCutter. There are a variety of sizes available. To make the projects in this book, I would recommend a 12" × 12" (30cm × 30cm) mat to use with the ShapeCutter and an 18" × 24" (46cm × 61cm) or 24" × 36" (61cm × 91cm) mat to use with the rotary cutter and the larger sheets of imported papers.

Brushes

The ¾-inch (19mm) wash brush is just the right size for applying laminate and découpage medium. In some cases a smaller brush will be needed to apply acrylic paint.

Scissors

An 8" (20cm) pair of multipurpose scissors and a smaller 5" (13cm) pair will be all that you need for any of the projects in this book. My favorite smaller scissors are Fiskars Softgrip Micro-Tip.

Decorative-Edge Scissors

There are many different decorative-edge scissors for papercrafting available. Each design adds something unique to a project. If I had to choose only one, I would choose the deckle blade because it looks old fashioned and works well with the vintage travel papers that are used for some of the Office Space projects.

Plastic Cups

A large supply of plastic cups will be useful. They are used many different times throughout this book to hold laminate, découpage medium, water, and as workstands for plates, lampshades and other pieces.

Paper Plates

I like to use paper plates for paint palettes. They hold a lot of paint and they do not require any cleanup!

Basic Techniques

There are several tools that I use in my studio that you will find very helpful when you are making the projects in this book. They will not only save time, but they will also help you achieve professional-looking results.

Using a Shape-Cutting Tool

The Fiskars ShapeCutter is the tool I use to make most of my shapes. To use the ShapeCutter, you will need a self-healing mat, a sharp blade and some shape templates. Always work on a flat surface and use templates that are designed for your particular cutter.

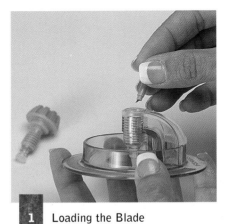

1 Loading the Blade

Unscrew and remove the orange knob. Drop the blade into the blade shaft.

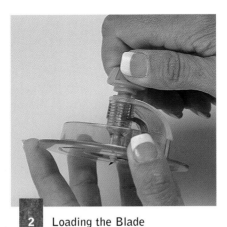

2 Loading the Blade

For template cutting, find the small indented band on the neck of the orange knob, just above the screw threads. Turn the knob until the top of the band is at the top of the blade shaft. All of the projects in this book use this setting. Adjust the blade slightly for thicker and thinner paper by turning the knob ¼ to ½ of a turn.

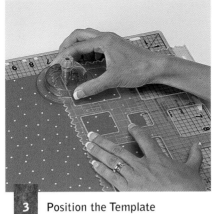

3 Position the Template

Lay your paper on a cutting mat, and set the template over the paper at the spot where you wish to cut the shape. For a square, start the cutter on one side, and not in a corner.

Outside of the Template

The cutter can be used to trace around the outside of the large templates as well as the inside. Simply apply a little pressure inward to keep the cutter next to the template. It may take a little bit of practice to get the feel for cutting on the template's perimeter, but it is well worth the time invested.

Cutting a Donut Shape

To create a donut shape with the cutter, always cut the inside (smaller) shape first. Be sure when you cut the first shape out that you have enough room around the paper for the larger shape. Position the larger template over the previously cut hole and cut out the larger shape.

Other Ways of Trimming Paper

In addition to the use of templates, you will want to familiarize yourself with the use of a rotary cutter and also the method of tearing paper to prepare it for application to a surface.

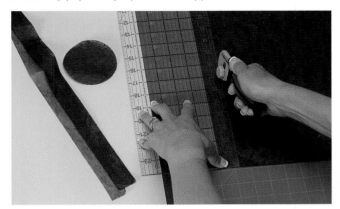

Rotary Cutter and Straightedge

Simply lay the straightedge over the paper at the desired measurement. Hold the straightedge firmly with one hand and set the rotary cutter blade next to the straightedge. Apply downward pressure to the cutter and run it along the straightedge.

Tearing Paper

If you are using one-sided paper, like scrapbook papers, you can create different deckle edges depending on how you tear the paper. If you want to create an edge that has a little bit of white showing, hold the portion of the paper that you wish to use, down with your left hand then tear the excess paper toward you with your right hand. For a tear with no white showing, hold the portion you're going to be using in your right hand, securing the excess flat on the table with your left hand and pull your right hand toward you. You can also achieve some interesting designs by incorporating both of these methods on the same paper.

Applying Mediums

The use of either découpage medium or liquid laminate will be explored in every project in this book, so it's worth mentioning some basic information about each of them. To achieve the best results, use the medium recommended in the materials list.

 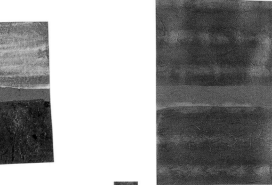

1 Mediums When Wet

Here is an example of the two mediums on different papers. The top of each paper was brushed with découpage medium and the lower part of each paper was brushed with laminate. Découpage is white and cloudy when applied and the laminate is clear and soaks into the paper. The laminate also turns the paper darker and in most cases the paper will stay darker as it dries. The purple paper is lightweight mulberry paper, and the teal paper is a heavier salago paper.

2 Mediums When Dry

This picture shows the same papers after they have dried. Both mediums dried clear and there is not much difference in color on the lightweight paper. However, note the color difference with the heavier paper.

Using Pour-On Poly Resin

This product is really fun to use. One coat gives your surface a very thick, durable, glass-like finish that is equal to about fifty coats of varnish! It works equally well on large and small projects and it will be used for several projects in this book. Envirotex is my product of choice. It is important to follow the directions carefully when you mix this product. I encourage you to read the instructions written by the manufacturer before you start. There is a guide in the instructions that will tell you how much Envirotex you will need for the surface area you are covering.

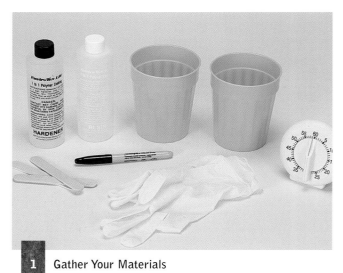

1 Gather Your Materials

You will need two plastic cups, a timer, craft sticks, rubber gloves, a bottle of resin, a bottle of hardener and a pen to mark the bottles. You will also want to protect your work surface with a disposable plastic cover.

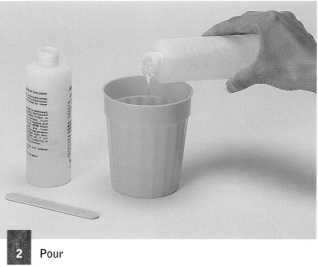

2 Pour

Pour an equal amount of resin and hardener into a plastic cup.

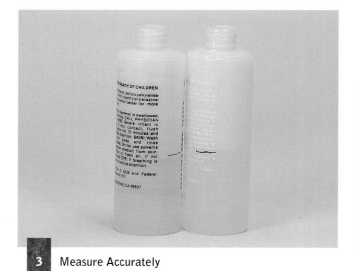

3 Measure Accurately

After you have poured the liquids, check the levels of each bottle to ensure you have used an equal amount of each. You can mark the bottles with the pen if needed.

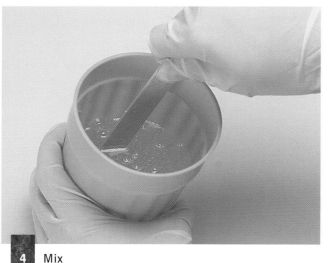

4 Mix

Whip the ingredients vigorously for one minute with a craft stick. Bubbles will begin to appear.

5 Pour Into a New Cup

To aid the mixing process, pour the mixture into a clean cup. Continue mixing vigorously for another full minute. The mixture will be full of bubbles and some of them will begin to float out of the cup as you mix. This is a good thing!

6 Pour Out the Mixture

Pour the mixture onto your surface. If the surface is large, pour the mixture in different areas instead of one large puddle. This will make it easier to spread.

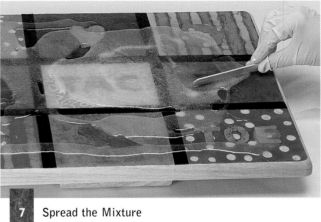

7 Spread the Mixture

Use a new craft stick to spread the mixture evenly over the surface. This step is like frosting a cake. Decide if you want the mixture to flow over the edges of your project or just stay on the surface. Do not worry about the bubbles.

8 Time for Five Minutes

Let the mixture sit for five minutes. Do not be tempted to cut this time short. This time allows the bubbles to rise to the surface.

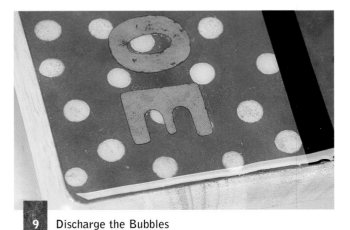

9 Discharge the Bubbles

After five minutes have past, gently exhale over the surface as if you were trying to fog up a window. You will see the bubbles instantly disappear. Continue breathing over the surface until all of the bubbles have disappeared.

living space

The projects in this chapter are designed for the formal living area of a home.

If you are like our family, we rarely utilize formal spaces in our home but they are the first rooms that you see when you come through the front door. Because they are rarely used, they are free of backpacks, shoes and discarded sports equipment! It is nice to have a place in your home that is tranquil, clutter-free and attractively decorated. These are the places that I escape to when I want a quiet place to read or drink a cup of coffee.

Having a few sophisticated art pieces in your formal spaces can make a bold decorating statement. In this chapter you will learn to make home decorating accessories including a lamp, a clock and a decorative screen to name just a few. All of these will add elegant style to your living space.

Blue and Green Lamp

Transform a plain fabric lampshade into an artsy paper shade that looks like it came from an expensive gallery. Beaded ribbon trim could be substituted for the eyelash trim for a completely different look.

MATERIALS

- six-panel lampshade
- white candlestick-style lamp base
- silver clips, square and S-shaped, 3 each
- green fringe trim
- blue eyelash fiber trim
- sheer blue ½" (12mm) ribbon
- purple thread
- liquid laminate
- ¼" (6mm) clear double-stick tape
- craft glue
- HeatnBond (heat-activated adhesive)
- scissors
- 2½" (6cm) circle template
- 1½" (4cm) circle template or ShapeCutter and Circles-1 template
- cutting mat
- tape measure
- ¾-inch (19mm) wash brush
- iron
- sewing needle
- two plastic cups

PAPER PALETTE

100% Kozo-Cobalt (Gold Leaf Paper Company)

Unryu-Forest Green (Black Ink)

Green swirls print fabric

Purple floral print fabric

Silver netting

✂ ABOUT THE PAPERS

The word Unryu means "cloud dragon paper" in Japanese and traditionally contains strands of fibers. The Unryu used here is made with strands of kozo which is a long rough fiber from a mulberry tree. We commonly refer to it as mulberry paper.

1 Tear and Add the Paper

Tear the blue paper into random-sized pieces. Brush a generous amount of liquid laminate onto the lampshade. Place a piece of paper on the shade and brush liquid laminate on the paper until it is saturated. Continue to cover the shade with the paper.

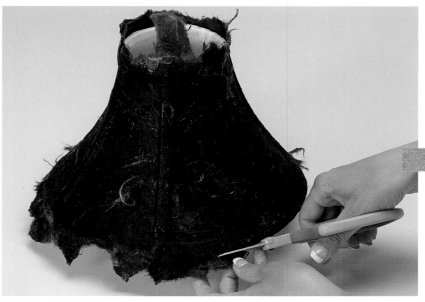

2 Trim the Edges

After the entire shade is covered with paper, press the paper over and into the ridges in the shade with your finger. While the paper is still wet, trim the excess paper off the top and bottom edges of the shade. Be careful not to cut the lining fabric of the shade as you trim the paper. Use the brush to apply more laminate to the trimmed edges and press with your fingers to make a strong bond to the shade.

3 Prepare Fabric for Cutting

Apply HeatnBond to the back of the two colors of fabric using an iron. This will stabilize the fabric, making it easier to cut shapes out of, with the ShapeCutter.

4 | Cut Circles From the Fabric

Cut out three 2½" (6cm) circles from each of the
purple and the green fabrics, using a template
and the ShapeCutter. Then cut out three of each
using a 1½" (4cm) circle template.

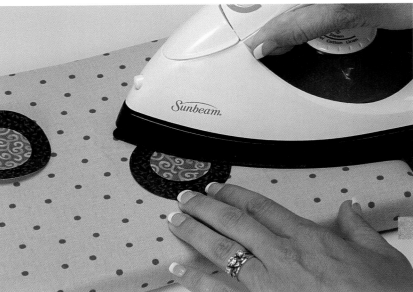

5 | Iron Small Circles to Large Circles

Peel the paper backing off the small circles.
Center one small circle onto each large circle,
pairing opposite colors together. Set the iron on
the circles and hold for a few seconds to bond.

6 | Sew on the Charms

Peel the backing off of the larger circles. Thread
the needle and begin sewing the wire charms to
the centers of the small circles. Sew the squares
onto the small green circles and the S shapes
onto the small purple circles. Tack each in about
three places.

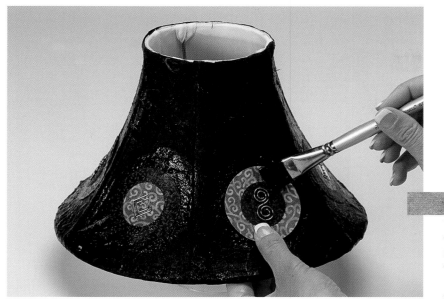

7   Adhere Shapes to the Shade

While the shade is still wet, center a fabric circle on the lower portion of one of the shade panels. Apply liquid laminate over the top of the circle with a brush until the fabric is saturated. Repeat this step for each of the fabric circles, alternating the colors around the shade.

8   Add the Blue Trim

After all of the circles are on, give the entire outside of the shade another coat of liquid laminate. Cut a length of the blue trim to fit around the bottom perimeter of the shade. Apply a thin coat of the laminate around the bottom edge of the shade and lightly adhere the trim to the wet laminate. You don't want all of the filaments to be stuck down. Let the shade dry.

9   Add the Green Trim

Cut a piece of green trim 1½" (4cm) longer than the perimeter of the top of the shade. Apply a bead of craft glue around the top of the shade and press the trim into the glue. Fold the extra trim under to create a finished edge.

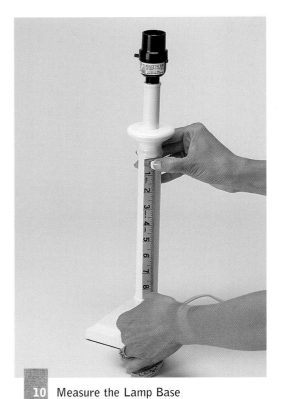

10 Measure the Lamp Base

Measure the height and the circumference of the candlestick portion of the lamp base.

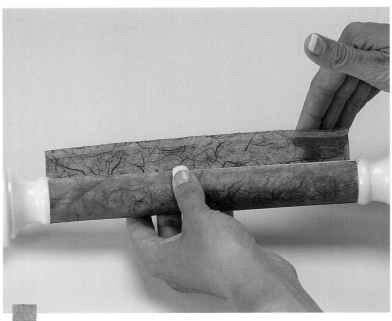

11 Cover the Base

Lay the silver mesh on top of the green mulberry paper. Cut the width of the paper ⅜" (10mm) larger than the circumference measurement. Then cut the length of the papers to equal the height measurement. Adhere a piece of double-stick tape to one long edge of the green paper. Wrap the green paper around the base of the lamp. Let the tape side of the paper overlap and stick to the other side of the paper. Repeat this step with the silver mesh.

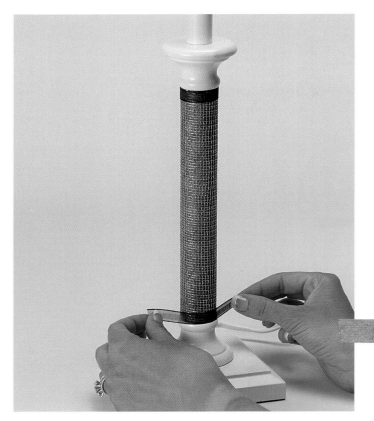

12 Add Ribbons to the Lamp Base

Cut two pieces of blue ribbon 1½" (4cm) longer than the circumference of the lamp base. Apply double-stick tape to the back side of each ribbon piece. Wrap the ribbons around the base at the top and bottom edges of the papers.

Mail Box

Start this project with a wooden mail box, cover it with paper and embellish it with fabric and metal shapes.
It coordinates very well with the blue and green lamp and may help organize all that junk mail.

Inspire Plaque

This is one of my favorite pieces in this book. The wooden clock base is covered with medium-weight textural paper. The paper molds easily to the shape of the wood when it is saturated with laminate. Add words that inspire you, a mini wire vase and a bouquet of curly sticks. This combination makes a unique art piece for your home.

MATERIALS

- wooden arch clock base (Walnut Hollow)
- blue or black acrylic mini frame set
- silver metal words: **Inspire** and **Imagine**
- silver swirl clip
- blue eyelets, four
- sprigs of purple and green curly grass
- silver metallic thread
- silver solder
- liquid laminate
- tape
- craft glue
- ¾-inch (19mm) wash brush
- wire cutter
- eyelet setting tool
- hammer
- protective surface
- sewing needle
- pencil
- plastic cup

PAPER PALETTE

Kozo-Cobalt (Gold Leaf Paper Company)

Olive felt

✂ ABOUT THE PAPERS

Kozo is of a heavier weight than the typical mulberry paper. The bottom side is smooth and the top side is very textural. Be sure to place the paper so that the textural, fiber side is up. The fibers are slightly lighter than the paper color which adds interest and dimension to the surface, so you don't want to hide it!

1 Cover the Base with Paper

Tear the blue paper into random-sized pieces. Brush liquid laminate onto the wooden clock base. Cover the entire clock base with paper except for the round feet. Saturate the paper pieces with laminate as you place them on the wooden base. The laminate will make the paper very pliable. Tear small pieces to fit around the corners and other small spaces. Use the end of the paintbrush to press the paper into the ridges along the sides and arch of the base.

2 Stitch Around the Frames

With the needle and silver thread, add a whipstitch around the two acrylic frames by inserting the needle through a hole from the front of the frame, bringing the thread around from the back of the frame and then inserting the needle through the front of the frame at the next hole.

3 Cut the Felt Pieces

Trace both of the frames on a piece of olive felt, using a pencil. Cut the felt pieces out.

4 Stitch the Swirl Clip

Stitch the square swirl clip to the center of the smaller piece of felt. Use a piece of metallic thread and a needle. Tack the clip to the felt in three places.

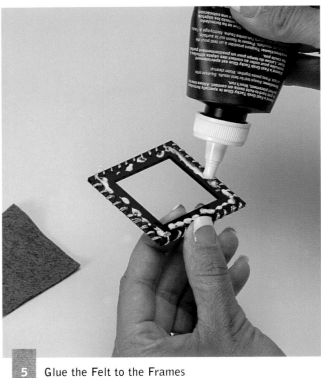

5 Glue the Felt to the Frames

Glue the felt pieces to the back of the acrylic frames. Glue the acrylic star in the center of the larger frame. Let dry.

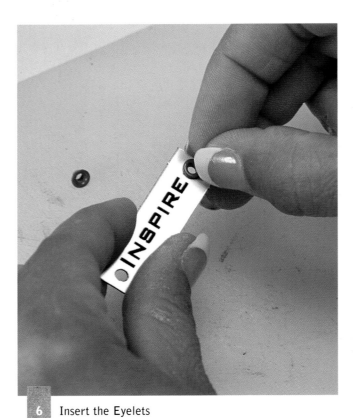

6 Insert the Eyelets

Set blue eyelets into each end of the silver words. Place the eyelet into the hole from the front and then turn the metal word over. Lay it onto a protective surface such as a piece of wood or cutting board.

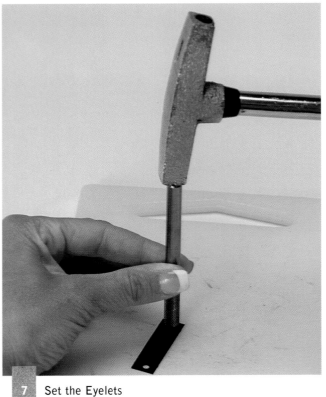

7 Set the Eyelets

Place the eyelet setting tool in the top of the eyelet shank. Tap the end of the setting tool with a hammer. This will spread and flatten the shank at the same time.

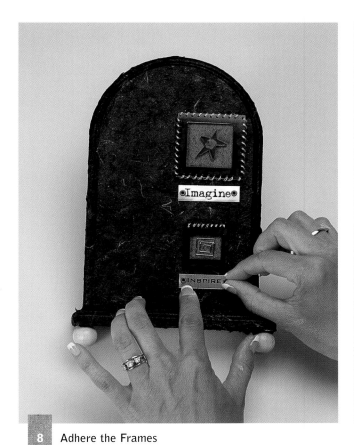

8 Adhere the Frames

Apply craft glue to the back of each frame and place them on the papered base. Glue the metal words under each of the frames.

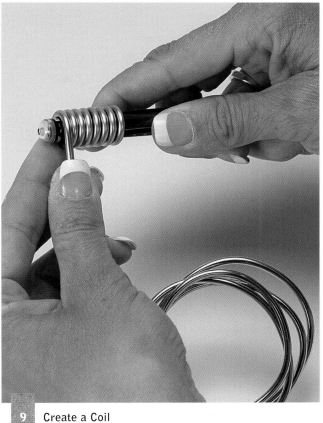

9 Create a Coil

Wrap the solder around the base of a pen to form a tight coil that is 1¾" (4cm) tall. Glue the coil to the bottom left side of the papered base.

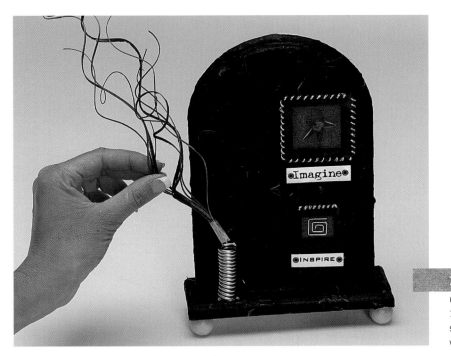

10 Add Curly Sprigs to the Coil

Cut several purple and green curly grass sprigs 10" (25cm) tall. Wrap the bottom ends of the sprigs with clear tape. Place the sprigs into the wire coil.

Striped Vase

This is an elegant vase that makes an impression. Its shape is simple and yet the bold paper stripes add sophistication and unexpected texture. Fill it with beautiful fresh flowers and make it a focal point in the entry area of your home.

MATERIALS

- glass vase, approximately 9" (23cm) tall × 19" (48cm) around at the widest point
- liquid laminate
- scissors
- rotary cutter
- cutting mat
- 24" (61cm) acrylic ruler
- tape measure
- ¾-inch (19mm) wash brush
- pencil
- plastic cup
- wire baking rack

PAPER PALETTE

Unryu-Forest (Black Ink)

Unryu-Purple (Black Ink)

ABOUT THE PAPERS

These lightweight Unryu papers (also known as mulberry paper) are translucent allowing the fibers from the mulberry tree to show through and add texture. They become very pliable when saturated with laminate.

1   Measure the Vase

Wrap a tape measure around the widest area of the vase to find the circumference. Divide the circumference by two. That will give you the number of paper strips you will need of each color. Next divide the circumference by the total number of strips. Then add ⅛" (3mm) to the measurement for overlap. This will be the width for the strips.

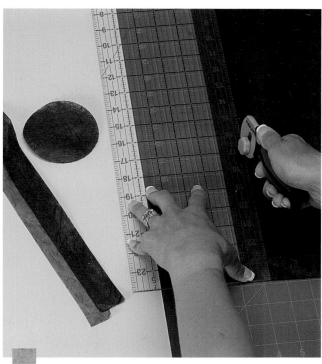

2   Cut the Strips

On the purple paper, trace a circle from the bottom of the vase and cut it out slightly smaller than the traced line. Use a rotary cutter and a ruler to cut your paper strips. Cut the length of the strips 1½" (4cm) longer than the height of the vase. If you have large sheets of paper, you can fold them in half and stack the green and purple paper together. This will insure the paper strips are the same width, and you will save time cutting several layers at once.

3   Begin Adding Green Strips

Brush a generous amount of liquid laminate onto a vertical section of the vase. Lay one green strip of paper on the vase. The paper should extend over both ends of the vase and should be perpendicular with the work surface. Apply liquid laminate to the paper until it is saturated. Smooth the paper into the curves of the vase with your finger. Repeat this step with a second green strip. Leave about 1" (3cm) or the equivalent of one paper strip width of space between the green strips at the widest section of the vase.

4 Adhere a Purple Strip

Lay a purple strip of paper between the two green strips. At the widest section of the vase the purple will slightly overlap the green on both sides. As the vase narrows, the purple will overlap more.

5 Continue Alternating Strips

Add another green strip and then a purple over the two green strips. Continue this process until the vase is covered. Adjust the spacing of the last few strips if necessary.

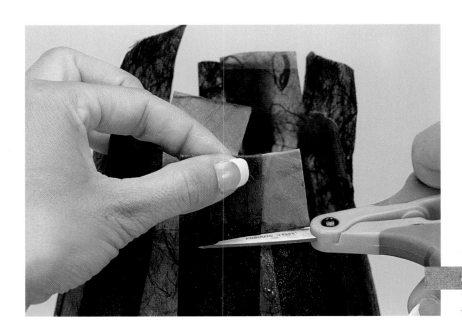

6 Trim Around the Rim

Trim the excess paper at the top of the vase so that each piece is even with the rim.

7 **Press the Edges Down**

Apply a little more laminate around the rim of the vase to help the paper adhere to the glass. Press the paper edges to the glass with your finger.

8 **Trim the Bottom**

Turn the vase up side down and trim the excess paper to overhang about 1" (3cm).

9 **Adhere the Paper to the Bottom**

Brush liquid laminate over the bottom of the vase. Fold the excess paper over the bottom of the vase and brush with laminate. Use your fingers to mold the paper over the base of the vase.

10 **Add the Circle**

Place the purple circle in the center of the bottom of the vase. Apply liquid laminate to the paper circle. Turn right side up on a wire baking rack to dry. Check the rim of the vase to be sure the paper is still securely bonded to the glass.

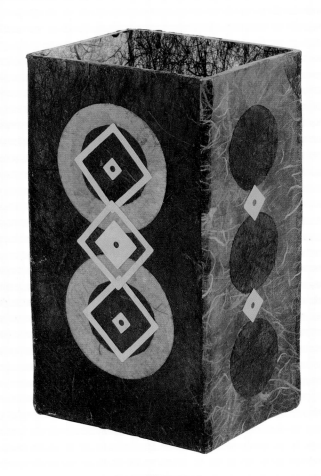

Embellished Vase

Any vase can be transformed with paper. This one was covered with purple and green mulberry paper and then embellished with gold, purple and green geometric shapes. Fill it with flowers or use it as a candle holder.

Green and Purple Plate

This plate was made with the same purple and green papers, but with the addition of silver swirl embellishments for a bit of sparkle. The plaid-like pattern adds a lot of interest as well.

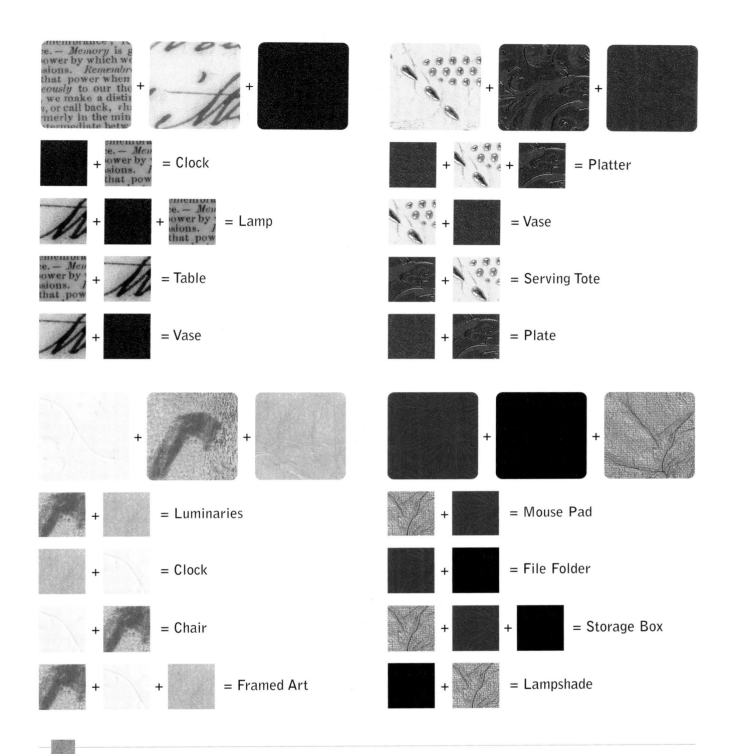

= Clock

= Lamp

= Table

= Vase

= Platter

= Vase

= Serving Tote

= Plate

= Luminaries

= Clock

= Chair

= Framed Art

= Mouse Pad

= File Folder

= Storage Box

= Lampshade

Three Papers, Endless Possibilities

The last three projects have had three colors in common and as you can see, it is easy to create multiple projects for any room that tie together with color and texture. Consider the suggestions above as a quick way to get you brainstorming about all of the endless (and easy!) ways to create a coordinated look to any number of objects.

Cigar Box Clock

I envision this clock on a fireplace mantel or adorning a beautiful writing desk or small accent table. The gold and black papers make a stunning combination. Find an interesting brass drawer pull for the top of the box.

MATERIALS

- wooden cigar box
- clock components
- gold drawer pull and screws (you will need shorter screws than the ones that come with the pull)
- brass metal corners, 4
- black number stickers
- wooden plugs for legs, 4
- black acrylic paint
- découpage medium
- craft glue
- ShapeCutter (or scissors)
- large circles template
- cutting mat
- acrylic ruler
- pencil
- ¾-inch (19mm) wash brush
- no. 10 shader brush
- drill
- small screwdriver

PAPER PALETTE

Black/Gold Stripe Silkscreen (Black Ink)

Black with Spirals (Black Ink)

Metallic-Gold (Black Ink)

✂ ABOUT THE PAPERS

The gold spirals and the black/gold stripe are Indian woodblock papers. The background paper is handmade and the design is hand-pressed onto the background with a carved wooden block.

1 Remove the Hardware

Remove the hinges and closure components from both ends of the box.

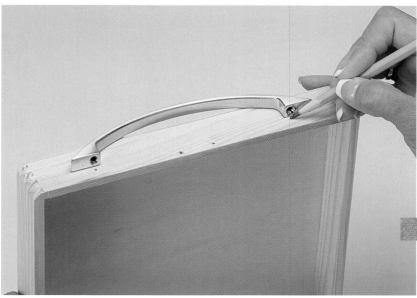

2 Mark the Hole Locations

Set the drawer pull on top of the wider half of the box. Center the handle and then lay it on its side. Mark the location for drilling the holes with a pencil.

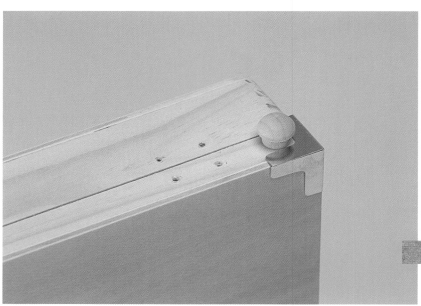

3 Adhere the Legs

Use a metal corner as a placement guide for the front two legs, and glue each of the four legs onto the bottom of the box.

4 Paint the Box

Paint both box halves, inside and out, with black acrylic paint using the no. 10 shader brush. Let the paint dry.

5 Apply Découpage Medium

Cover the box halves with découpage medium, using the ¾-inch (19mm) wash brush. This will protect the paint. Set aside to dry.

6 Cut Out the Shapes

Use the 6" (15cm) circle template and the ShapeCutter to cut a circle from the gold paper. With the 4½" (11cm) circle template, cut a circle from the Black with Spirals paper. Trace around the front half of the box with a pencil, onto the black and gold striped paper. Be sure the lines are vertical and square with the box. Cut out this shape.

7 Adhere the Paper Shapes

Cover the front of the box with découpage medium using the ¾-inch (19mm) wash brush. Lay the striped paper on the front of the box so that all the edges are aligned. Smooth out the paper working from the center to the outside edges. Apply another coat of découpage medium over the entire surface of the striped paper. Lay the gold circle in the center of the box and press it smooth. Cover the gold circle with découpage medium and lay the smaller circle in the center. Smooth out that circle and apply a coat of découpage medium over the entire surface of the box. Allow it to dry completely.

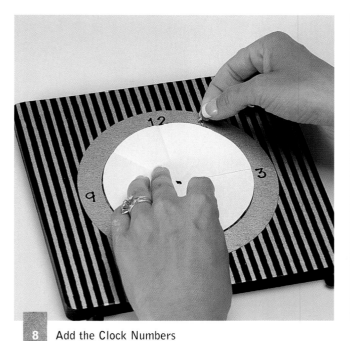

8 Add the Clock Numbers

Cut another 4½" (11cm) circle from a piece of scrap paper. Fold it into eighths. Cut a small hole in the center of the circle. Place the circle on top of the spiral circle. Mark the center of the circle on the box. Drill a hole in the center at this mark with a ⁵⁄₁₆" (8mm) bit. Set the scrap paper back on the swirl circle and use the fold lines as a guide for placing the self-adhesive numbers. Start with the 12, 6, 3 and 9. Place the other numbers evenly between the other fold lines.

9 Add the Clock Components

Push the clock shaft through the hole in the box from back to front. Add the washer, hex nut and hands to the shaft.

10 Reattach the Hardware

Reattach the hinges and closure components to the box. Add the drawer pull to the top of the box.

11 Add the Metal Hardware

Attach the metal corners to the front of the box with craft glue.

Embossed Bowl

Can this really be a paper bowl? It is indeed and I love the understated elegance of the embossing.
The paper is molded to form the shape of a bowl. This bowl would be a perfect accent for a coffee table.

MATERIALS

- foam balls, 3" (8cm)
- liquid laminate
- paper glaze
- fabric stiffener
- rotary cutter
- cutting mat
- ruler
- pencil
- ¾-inch (19mm) wash brush
- spray bottle
- hair dryer
- glass bowl (for form)
- plastic cup
- cup of water

PAPER PALETTE

Embossed
Daisies-Iris
(Black Ink)

Indian Dewdrop-
Silver on Royal Blue
(Black Ink)

Kilim-Periwinkle
(Black Ink)

Napa-Purple
(Black Ink)

ABOUT THE PAPERS

The embossed daisy paper is made in Thailand and looks like it is made out of cotton but the fiber is actually Kozo, or mulberry. A chalky gray/blue color has been added to the raised areas. The Indian dewdrop paper is made from cotton and has raised silver dots that look like drops of solder. The Napa paper is tissue weight and has vines of gold screenprinted on the purple background. The Kilim paper is handmade and the design is pressed onto the background with a wood block.

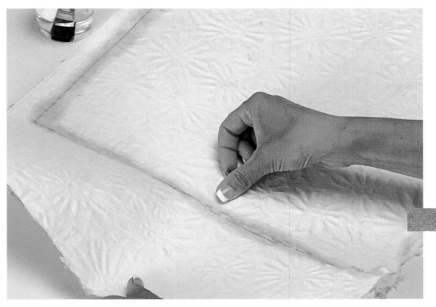

1 Tear the Paper

Mark a 15" (38cm) square on the back of the embossed paper with a pencil. Trace along the pencil line with a water-filled brush. Create a water line about ¾" (19mm) wide. Gently tear along the pencil line to create a deckled edge.

2 Saturate the Paper

Pour the fabric stiffener into a spray bottle. Spray the back of the paper with stiffener. Apply enough stiffener to make the paper pliable.

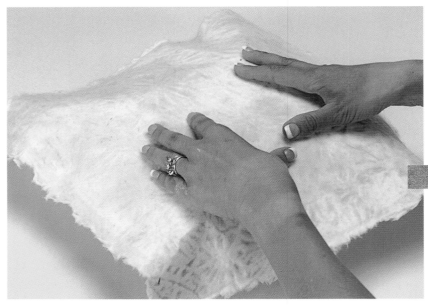

3 Form the Bowl Shape

Place the glass bowl upside down on top of a plastic cup. Lay the paper face down over the glass bowl. Mold the paper over the back of the bowl with your hands. Spray the paper with additional stiffener as needed to shape the paper over the bowl. Quickly dry the paper with a hair dryer. Spray the paper a second time and dry with the hair dryer.

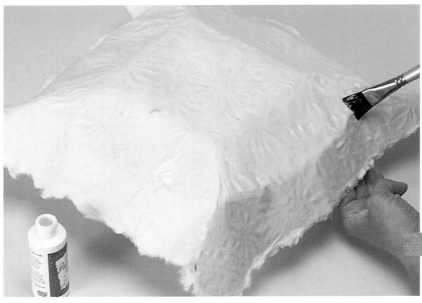

4   Coat the Bowl with Paper Glaze

Apply two generous coats of paper glaze to the back of the paper bowl. Let the glaze dry between coats.

5   Apply Glaze to the Inside

Turn the glass bowl right side up. Place the paper bowl inside the glass bowl. Apply two coats of paper glaze to the inside of the bowl. Let the glaze dry between coats.

6   Adhere Paper Strips to Foam Ball

Cut strips approximately ⅜" × 5" (1cm × 13cm) from one of the blue papers. Brush liquid laminate over one of the foam balls. Lay the first paper strip on the ball and brush it with laminate. Lay the second paper strip on the opposite side of the first, starting and ending at the same point. Continue adding strips of paper around the ball, saturating the paper as you go.

7 Continue Covering the Ball

Begin to fill in the spaces between the first strips of paper. Cut some of the strips shorter to fill in as the strips get closer together.

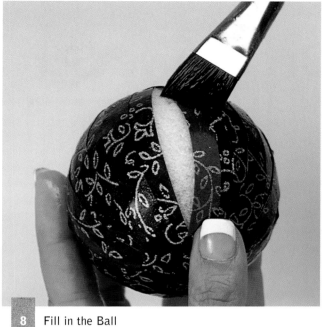

8 Fill in the Ball

Continue adding strips until the ball is completely covered. Smooth the paper strips with your finger so all of the paper edges are securely bonded to the ball. Repeat for the other papers and foam balls. Set the balls in the finished bowl for display.

Blue Bowl

This bowl was formed around a plastic freezer container! The paper was draped over the sides and onto the work surface. The edges were ruffled and then dried with a blow dryer. After it was dry, I trimmed the edges with decorative scissors and covered it with several coats of paper glaze.

Decorative Screen

This is one of the easiest projects in this book, but at the same time, delivers the most decorative impact. A screen can add interest to any corner or room in your home. You can create separation between two living spaces or add a backdrop for other decorative accessories. This is the perfect size for a fireplace or a window screen. For a larger screen simply increase the size of the wood frame.

MATERIALS

- cabinet frames, 13" × 30" (33cm × 76cm), 2
- cabinet frame, 21" × 30" (53cm × 76cm)
- brass hinges with screws, 4
- wood stain (mahogany)
- craft glue
- rotary cutter
- cutting mat
- straightedge
- pencil
- tape measure
- screwdriver
- cloth rag
- rubber gloves

PAPER PALETTE

Chainlinks-Olive/Gold/Copper (Black Ink)

Kilim-Olive/Green (Black Ink)

Mango-Olive (Black Ink)

Riviere-Sand (Black Ink)

Woodgrain-Beige/Olive (Black Ink)

✂ ABOUT THE PAPERS

Chainlinks is a handmade paper from India. Gold and copper threads are machine sewn into the paper to create design and texture. Riviere is made in Japan and the design is created with small fibers that are laid over the top of the base paper. In this case the fibers are the same color as the base paper making the design very subtle. I think this particular design looks like hammered metal.

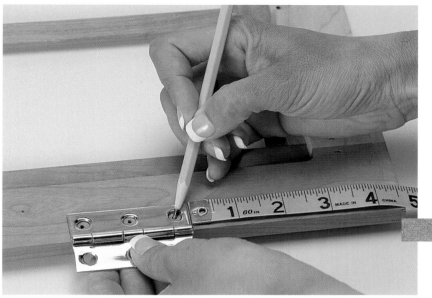

1 Mark the Hinges

Mark the holes for the hinges on all three cabinet pieces, placing each hinge about 4" (10cm) from the top and bottom edges of the frames.

2 Apply Stain

Apply mahogany stain to all of the frames with a cloth rag. I prefer gel stain because it is easier to use. It is thicker so it does not run and you can control the color better.

3 Cut the Panel Papers

Measure the top, bottom and center sections of all three frames. See diagrams 2 and 3 on page 123 for measuring guidelines. Cut out the papers following diagram 1 on page 123.

4 Adhere Paper to the Side Panels

Run a light bead of craft glue around the bottom section of one side panel. Smooth the bead of glue with your finger. Lay a piece of Chainlinks paper over the bottom panes. Press the paper into the glue with your finger.

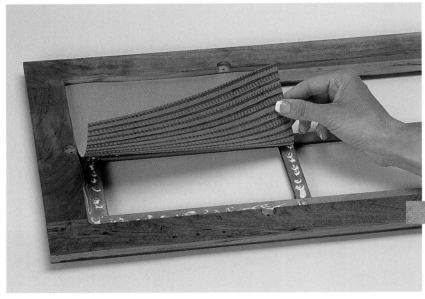

5 Adhere the Second Paper

Apply glue to the top panes of the same side panel and lay a piece of Kilim paper over the top section. Press the paper into the glue with your finger. Repeat steps four and five for the other side panel.

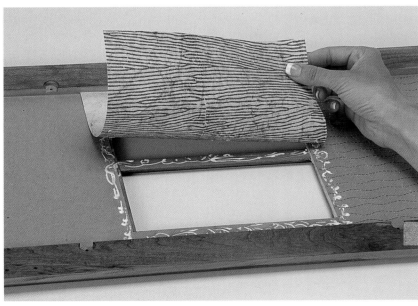

6 Add the Center Paper to one Side Panel

Apply glue on top of the upper and lower papers and in the interior frame. Align and lay the Woodgrain paper in place. Press the paper down with your finger.

7 | **Add the Center Paper to the Second Side Panel**

Add the Woodgrain paper to the center of the other side panel. Set the panels aside to dry.

8 | **Add Paper to the Middle Panel**

Glue the Riviere paper to the center section of the middle panel. Glue the Mango paper to the center top and center bottom sections of the panel. Glue the three other papers to the panel over the top of the middle papers. The Kilim will go on top, the Chainlinks on the bottom, and the Woodgrain in the center. See the diagram on page 123 for measuring help.

9 | **Assemble the Screen**

Lay the screens face down in order of sequence. Place the hinges in the locations that you previously marked. Screw the brass hinges to the panels. You may want to predrill the holes to prevent the wood frame from splitting.

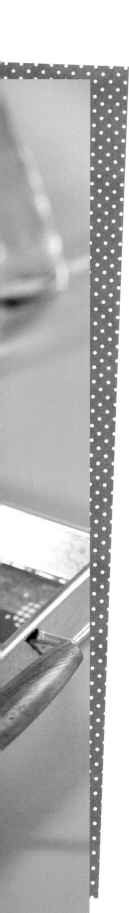

dining
space

By now you've seen that paper can perform in amazing ways, from a lampshade to a vase. We've even used paper to create a decorative bowl, but I'll bet you never imagined using paper as a prime element in the dining room, right?

You may not think paper is durable enough to use in your dining room, but you will learn in this chapter how to create projects that are beautiful, functional, decorative and durable. Ordinary plates, trays, candlesticks, coasters and glasses are transformed with the help of beautiful decorative papers.

Autumn Plate

You can create a plate for all four seasons with this simple laminating technique. Use your imagination and find unique paper shapes, flat ornaments, ribbons and other embellishments for your plate. A plate decorated in this way should always be washed by hand.

MATERIALS

- 11" (28cm) clear glass square plate
- paper leaves
- gold micro beads
- liquid laminate
- paper glaze
- scissors
- ¾-inch (19mm) wash brush
- plastic cups

PAPER PALETTE

Mango-Brick
(Black Ink)

Mango-Brown
(Black Ink)

Mango-Mustard
(Black Ink)

Mango-Rust
(Black Ink)

✂ ABOUT THE PAPERS
The papers used in this project are colored mulberry with inclusions of mango leaves. The mango leaves add a rich texture to the paper. They are machine made in Thailand but have a wonderful handmade feel.

1 Arrange the Leaves

Lay the plate right side up and arrange the leaves under the plate so you can see what they look like. Arrange the leaves so some are going off the edge of the plate. Set the leaves to the side in the pattern that you want for the plate. Turn the plate upside down (on top of one or two plastic cups, if you like). Brush the back of the plate with liquid laminate and begin to place the leaves face down on the plate.

GIRL'S NIGHT OUT
Host a girlfriend get-together. You provide the plates and have everyone else bring different papers and accessories to share with the other guests. At the end of the evening, everyone will have a unique treasure to take home with them.

2 Adhere the Leaves

Brush the back of the leaves with laminate and smooth with your fingers. Press the corners of the leaves down to form tightly to the shape of the plate.

THREE-DIMENSIONAL TEXTURE
Micro beads are just one type of embellishment that could be used with a clear glass plate. Consider skeleton leaves, wire swirls, die-cut letters, sand, metallic confetti or even metal washers.

3 Add the Micro Beads

Trim the leaves that are over the edges with scissors. While the liquid laminate is still wet, sprinkle the back of the plate with gold micro beads. Add a bit more laminate if necessary. The bead placement can be fairly random.

4 Apply Liquid Laminate

Brush the excess beads off the back of the leaves. Tear the mulberry papers into random sizes. Apply the laminate directly to the paper pieces before you put them on the plate. Use the ¾"-inch (19mm) wash brush to apply the laminate. Lay the laminated paper piece on the back of the plate.

5 Add the Remaining Paper

Continue adding pieces of mulberry paper in random color patterns. Let the papers go over the edges of the plate. When the entire plate is covered, trim the excess paper from the edges. Press the edges of the plate with your finger to ensure the paper is firmly bonded to the glass. Set aside to dry. Brush the back of the plate with a generous coat of paper glaze.

Spring Plate

The paper flowers were the inspiration for this spring plate. Arrange the flowers on your work surface until you have the pattern that you are happy with. Cover the back of the plate with laminate and begin applying the flowers to the plate. Cover the flowers with three layers of purple tissue paper. Apply the tissue paper one sheet at a time.

Summer Plate

To create this plate, I covered it with polka dot tissue paper and then added a layer of gold tissue paper. This is so easy . . . just look for interesting tissue paper in the gift wrap area of your favorite store.

Winter Plate

The snowflakes for this plate were punched out of gold moiré paper and the other shapes were either cut or punched out of gold holographic paper. Use this design to make plates for your holiday table, or fill them with goodies for your next cookie exchange. Remember they are beautiful and functional!

Retro Tray

Functional and fun! Transform a simple tray into a fabulously trendy serving piece. Combine it with the candlesticks on page 56 and create an attractive focal point for your table. Use the tray for serving or fill it with votives of differing heights for a centerpiece in your dining room or on your patio. You may find some of the materials for this project in your scrapbooking supplies. That's right, the papers used to make this tray are scrapbook papers. Think of the possibilities!

MATERIALS

- galvanized tray
  10½" × 14¼" (27cm × 36cm)
  (inside measurements)
- brown paint (Delta No
  Primer Metal)
- découpage medium
- Envirotex Lite poly resin
- scissors
- 2" (5cm) circle template
- 1" (3cm) circle template
- 2" (5cm) square template
  or ShapeCutter and
  Circles-1, Squares-1
- cutting mat
- ¾-inch (19mm) wash brush
- gloves
- wooden craft sticks
- two plastic cups

PAPER PALETTE

Red Gingham
(Karn Foster
Designs)

Red Polka Dot
(Karn Foster
Designs)

Small Dots on
Bright Red
(The Paper Patch)

Small Red Checks

White Random
Dots on Red
(The Paper Patch)

✂ ABOUT THE PAPERS

These are scrapbook papers that you can find in any craft or specialty scrapbook store. Look for papers that have varying sizes of dots and checks. The color combination of the tan and red gives this project a "retro" look.

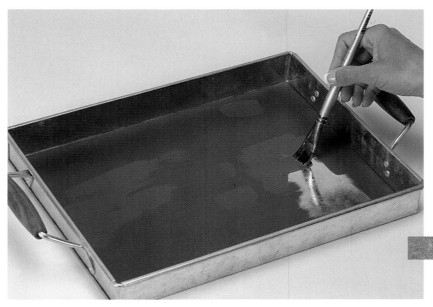

1 Paint the Tray Bottom

Apply a coat of the brown metal paint to the bottom of the inside of the tray. Set it aside to dry overnight.

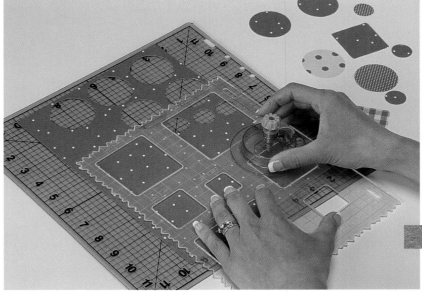

2 Cut Out the Shapes

Using the ShapeCutter or scissors and templates, cut out paper circles and squares. See chart and diagram on page 55 for shape and layout details.

3 Adhere the First Rows of Squares

Arrange the paper shapes in a grid beside the tray. Use découpage medium to apply one vertical row and one horizontal row. These rows will set the spacing for the other papers.

4 **Add the Remaining Shapes**

Continue to apply the squares and the larger circles. Apply the small circles last. Coat all the paper with a generous amount of découpage medium. Be sure that all edges of the papers are sealed with découpage. After it has dried, apply a second coat of découpage medium. The second coat is very important and will prevent the Envirotex from seeping under the papers so don't be tempted to skip this step.

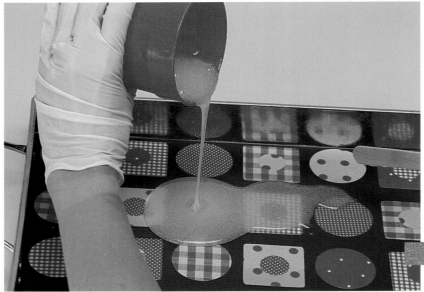

5 **Pour on the Clear Coat**

Prepare a batch of Envirotex (see page 14) and pour it over the découpaged papers.

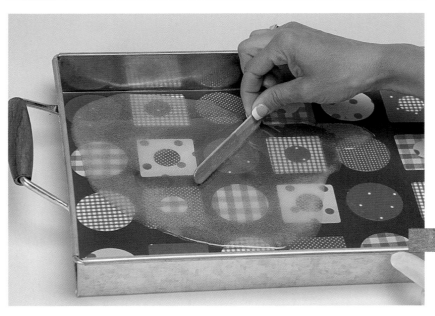

6 **Spread the Mixture**

Spread the mixture with a craft stick as evenly as possible over the surface. Let it stand for five minutes and then discharge the bubbles as described on page 15. Set aside to cure.

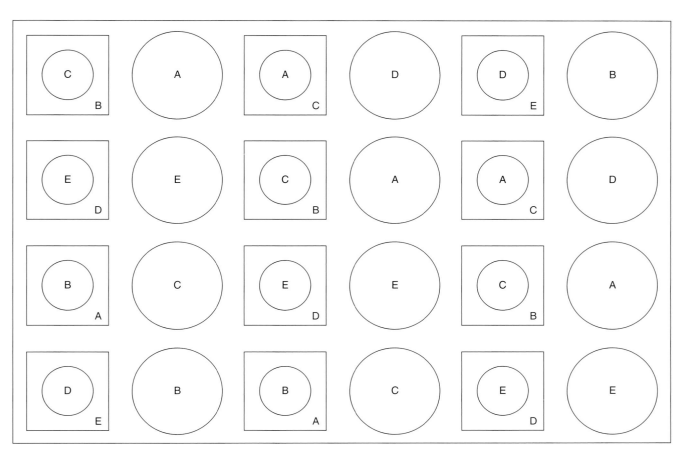

Layout grid of papers

![icon] **Paper Shapes**

Red Gingham (A)	2" squares, two
	2" circles, three
	1" circles, three
Red Polka Dot (B)	2" squares, two
	2" circles, three
	1" circles, two
Small Dots (C)	2" squares, three
	2" circles, two
	1" circles, two
Small Checks (D)	2" squares, three
	2" circles, two
	1" circles, two
Random Dots (E)	2" squares, two
	2" circles, two
	1" circles, three

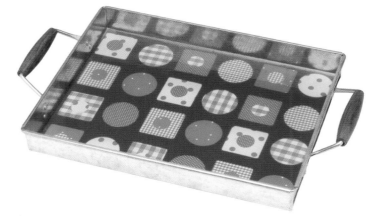

Retro Candlesticks

Although the glass jars are inexpensive, they can be turned into one-of-a-kind, decorative pieces for your table and take just minutes to make!

MATERIALS

- square, corked glass jars, 2
- red candles, 2
- scrapbook paper (see Retro Tray, p. 52)
    Small Red Checks
    Red Polka Dot
- brown text-weight paper
- découpage medium
- rotary cutter
- scissors
- 4" (10cm) square template
- 3½" (9cm) circle template
- 3" (7cm) circle template
    or ShapeCutter and
    Large 4" (10cm) square
    Circles-1
- cutting mat
- acrylic ruler
- ¾-inch (19mm) wash brush

1 Cut Out Shapes and Adhere

Cut one square of the check paper and one square of the dot paper using the ShapeCutter and the 4" (10cm) template. Cut out two brown 3½" (9cm) circles, one checked 3" (7cm) circle, and one spotted 3" (7cm) circle using the Circles-1 template. Apply découpage medium to the back of the squares and center one on each of the jars. Smooth the papers from the center out. Découpage a brown circle to the center of each paper square.

2 Add Paper Around the Neck

Découpage the 3" (7cm) checked and spotted circles to the center of the brown circles. Cut two strips of brown paper ½" × 4" (12cm × 10cm) and two red spotted strips ¼" × 4" (6mm × 10cm) using the rotary cutter and a ruler. Apply découpage medium to the back of one of the brown strips of paper and wrap it around the neck of one jar. Apply découpage to the back of one red paper strip and wrap it around the center of the brown strip. Repeat for the other jar. Remove the corks from the jars and place a candle in each opening.

Retro Coasters

With the help of a heavy-duty, clear-coat finish, papier-mâché discs become fabulous retro coasters. The clear coat looks like glass and adds durability. Find other interesting papier-mâché shapes and add them to your coaster collection.

MATERIALS

- 3¾" (10cm) papier-mâché circles, set of four
- scrapbook paper (see Retro Tray, p. 52)
    - Small Red Checks
    - Red Polka Dot
- brown text-weight paper
- Primary Red acrylic paint (Delta)
- découpage medium
- Envirotex Lite
- scissors
- 3½" (9cm) circle template
- 3" (7cm) circle template or ShapeCutter and Circles-1
- cutting mat
- ¾-inch (19mm) wash brush
- gloves
- wooden craft sticks
- two plastic cups

1 Adhere Shapes to Coasters

Paint the coasters red and set them aside to dry. Cut out four 3½" (9cm) brown circles, two 3" (7cm) check circles and two 3" (7cm) spotted circles. Cover the top of the coasters with découpage medium and then place a brown circle in the center of each coaster. Center a red print paper on the top of each of the brown circles and découpage them in place. Let dry. Apply a second coat of medium to each coaster, taking care to seal all the paper edges well. Let dry.

2 Pour on Clear Coat

Set the coasters on a spool of thread or small flat object. Mix up a small batch of Envirotex (see page 14) and pour it over the coasters.

3 Spread Mixture Evenly

Use a craft stick to spread the mixture evenly. Follow the instructions for discharging bubbles on page 15. Set the coasters aside to cure.

Curvy Votive Holders

I just had to smile when I found these funky vases. Their curvy shapes add a bit of whimsy and a whole lot of character. Simply cover them with mulberry paper, add some crystal embellishments and you have an attractive centerpiece for your table. Make a grouping of six or seven, and they can line the center of your dining table, light up your kitchen window sill or add interest to a buffet table.

MATERIALS

- curvy glasses, 2 (different heights)
- acrylic jewel crystals, mixture of ¼" (6mm) and ⅜" (10mm)
- liquid laminate
- decorative punches:
    sun— ⅝" (16mm)
    dot— ⅝" (16mm)
    swirl—1¼" (3cm)
- scissors
- pencil
- ¾-inch (19mm) wash brush

PAPER PALETTE

Salago-Grape
(Black Ink)

Salago-Mediterranean
(Black Ink)

Unryu-Fuchsia

Unryu-Teal

✂ ABOUT THE PAPERS

Salago is a wild shrub similar to the Japanese mulberry tree. Salago paper is heavier in weight than mulberry paper and is handmade in the Philippines. The heavier weight paper works better for punching out shapes. These papers also have inclusions of coconut, rice hulls, abaca fibers or banana bark.

1 Punch the Shapes

Using the decorative punches, cut out several swirls from the grape paper and several dots and suns from the blue Salago paper.

2 Adhere the Dots and Suns

Apply liquid laminate with the wash brush to the outside of the taller glass. Place the blue dots and suns about 2" (5cm) apart in a random pattern around the glass. Saturate each of the shapes with more laminate.

3 Tear and Adhere the Teal paper

Tear the teal mulberry paper into small random-sized pieces. While the liquid laminate is still wet, begin to cover the glass with mulberry paper. Use the wash brush to saturate each piece of paper as you apply it to the glass. Brush the pieces of paper under the bottom of the glass. Let the papers at the top of the glass extend past the rim of the glass.

4 **Adhere the Swirls**

Apply liquid laminate to the outside of the smaller glass, using the wash brush and adhere the swirls in a random pattern, spacing the pieces about 1½" (4cm) apart.

5 **Repeat with the Fuchsia Paper**

Repeat step 4, using fuchsia mulberry to cover the smaller glass.

6 **Trim the Edges**

Trim the excess paper from the tops of the glasses. Smooth the edges of the paper against the top of the glasses to ensure a firm bond.

7 **Trace the Circles**

Trace the bottom of each glass onto its corresponding paper and cut out the circles with scissors, cutting the shapes just slightly smaller than the traced line.

8 Laminate the Paper Circles

Brush liquid laminate to the bottom of the teal glass. Center the teal paper circle on the bottom of the glass and saturate it with laminate. Repeat for the fuchsia glass and set both glasses aside to dry.

9 Add the Crystals

Adhere crystals to each of the glasses randomly with tacky glue.

Polka Dots Serving Platter

This beautiful platter can be used as a serving tray or as a decorative art piece for your home. It looks very elegant on a plate stand or hanging on a wall but it's also functional. The back of the plate is covered with paper and a glaze finish is added for durability. Use it to serve cookies, appetizers or cucumber sandwiches. The front surface of the platter can be hand washed. For companion pieces, make additional plates with other geometric shapes such as squares, triangles or diamonds.

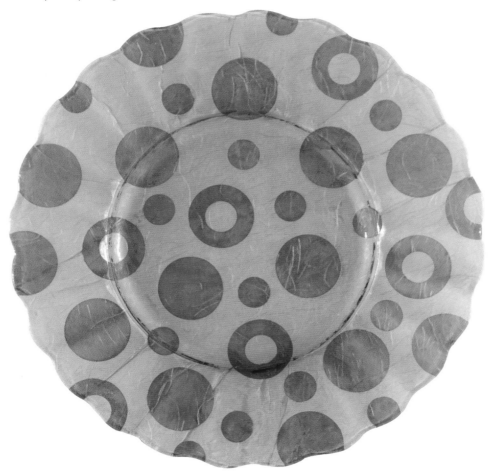

MATERIALS

- 15" (38cm) scalloped platter
- liquid laminate
- paper glaze
- scissors
- 2" (5cm) circle template
- 1" (3cm) circle template or ShapeCutter and Circles-1 template
- cutting mat
- pencil
- ¾-inch (19mm) wash brush
- plastic cups

PAPER PALETTE

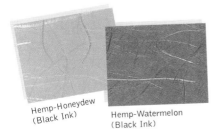

Hemp-Honeydew (Black Ink)

Hemp-Watermelon (Black Ink)

✂ ABOUT THE PAPERS

These papers are made in Japan and have strands of manila hemp scattered over the surface of the paper. The hemp catches the light and makes the paper look like it has silk threads in it. Notice that the fibers are only on one side of the paper. I love the combination of these two colors.

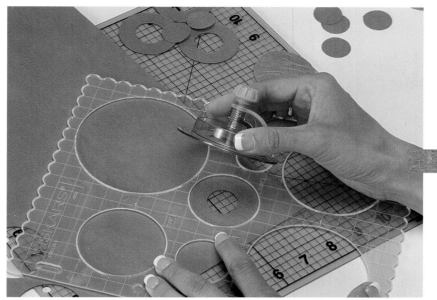

1 Cut Out the Circles

Use the ShapeCutter and the Circles-1 template to cut out the following shapes from the watermelon paper. Cut out thirteen 2" (5cm) circles. Cut out eleven 1" (3cm) circles, spacing them at least 3" (8cm) apart on the large sheet of paper. Cut out six donut shapes by placing the 2" (5cm) template over the top of a 1" (3cm) hole that was left in the large sheet of paper (see Cutting a Donut Shape, page 12).

2 Trace the Plate

Turn the honeydew paper face down and set the plate face down on top of it. Trace the perimeter of the plate with a pencil, then measure out about 1" (3cm) from that line and cut out the circle, using scissors.

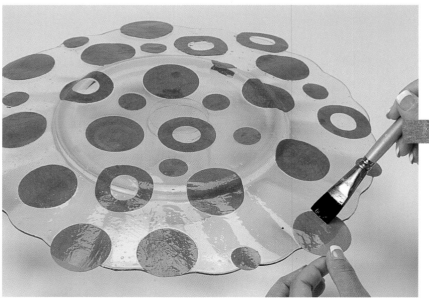

3 Adhere the Circles

Turn the plate upside down on top of a plastic cup. Use the wash brush to cover the back of the plate with liquid laminate. Arrange the circles in a random pattern on the back of the plate. Be sure to place the circles hemp side down so the fibers can be seen from the front of the plate. Place some of the circles so they extend over the edge of the plate. Brush liquid laminate on the back of each circle so it is saturated. Trim away any of the circle pieces that hang over the edge of the plate.

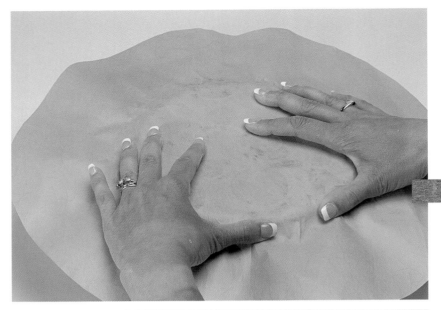

4 Add the Honeydew Paper

Apply a generous coat of liquid laminate over the entire surface of the back of the plate. Place the honeydew paper face down on the back of the plate. Apply laminate to the paper and press the paper firmly to the glass. Begin to smooth and mold the paper to the plate starting in the center and working your way toward the outside edges.

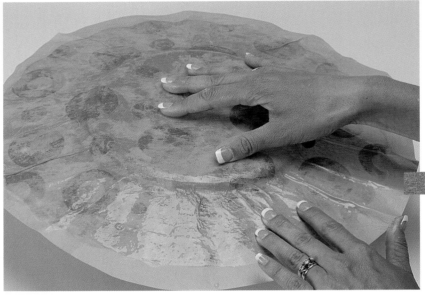

5 Continue Molding the Paper

Brush more laminate over the back of the paper to keep it pliable. Use your fingers to mold the paper into the scalloped areas of the plate. Don't worry if you have a few wrinkles in the paper. Smooth them the best you can and the remaining wrinkles are what I call "handmade nuances," and will barely be seen on the front of the plate.

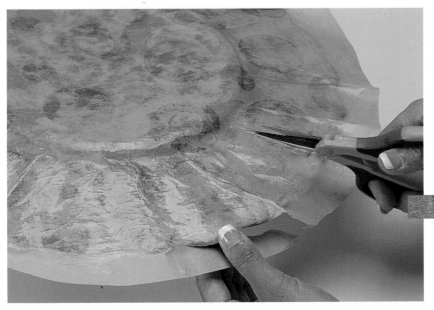

6 Trim the Excess Paper

Trim the excess paper off the edges of the plate with scissors. Press the edges of the paper firmly to the glass. Let the laminate dry. Apply a coat of paper glaze to finish the back of the plate. Apply one or two additional coats of glaze if you will be using the plate as a serving platter.

Martini Glass

Use this glass as a companion to the Polka Dots Platter to create a chip and dip set. Simply place the glass in the center of the platter and fill it with your favorite vegetable or chip dip. Or, make several of these glasses and line them up in the center of your table. Fill them with tea candles, and they become elegant votives.

MATERIALS

- martini glass
- Hemp–Honeydew paper (see Polka Dots Serving Platter, page 62)
- liquid laminate
- scissors
- 1½" (4cm) circle template
- 1" (3cm) circle template or ShapeCutter and Circles-1 template
- cutting mat
- ¾-inch (19mm) wash brush

1   Cut Out and Add Circles

Using the same method to cut circles as you did in the first step of the plate, cut out six solid 1" (3cm) circles and seven 1½" (4cm) donuts from the Honeydew paper. Brush liquid laminate over the base of the glass, using the wash brush, and randomly place some of the circles. Trim the circles that extend over the edge of the base. Set aside to dry.

2   Repeat for the Bowl of the Glass

Cover the outside of the bowl with liquid laminate. Add paper circles in a random pattern. If needed, trim a circle to fit around the glass stem where it attaches to the bowl. Trim away the circles that extend over the edge of the glass. Brush away drips that may form while the glass is drying.

LAY IT ON THICK

It's better to apply one thick coat of liquid laminate than to overwork several thinner coats. One solution for drips is to wipe them with a dry brush. Start the brushstroke at the base of the bowl and move toward the rim. This will remove the drips, and the glass will appear to have crystal-like lines in it.

kid
space

The projects in this chapter were truly inspired by the brightly colored papers.

Stripes and polka dots come together to create whimsical, kid-friendly, eye-popping accessories that children of all ages will adore. I knew that I was on the right track when my thirteen-year-old daughter came into my studio and said, "Mom, these are cool!" I take that as high praise.

Kids and paper you say? How can that be practical? This chapter will show you how to make paper a practical and functional decorating medium for your child's room. Include your child in the creative process, and when you are finished creating. . . how about a game of tic-tac-toe?

Color Block Panels

Canvas boards are versatile decorating items. They come in a variety of sizes and shapes and can make a big impact without blowing your budget. The bold color blocks will add a dramatic flair to any room.

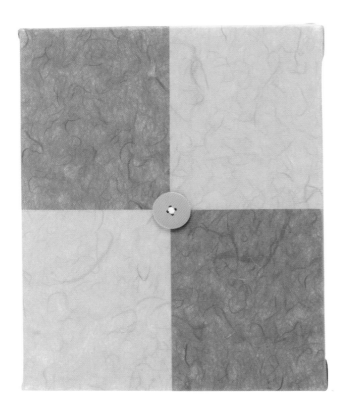
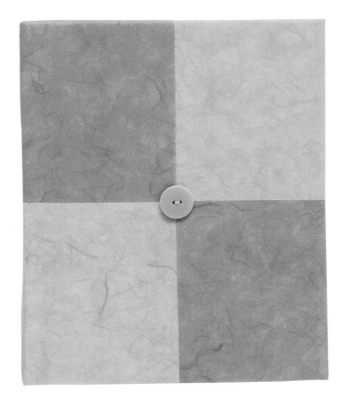

MATERIALS

- 8" × 10" (20cm × 25cm) pre-stretched canvases, 2
- brightly colored buttons, 2
- brightly colored embroidery floss
- double-stick tape
- spray adhesive
- glue dots
- rotary cutter
- cutting mat
- ruler
- pencil
- needle
- protective surface for spraying

PAPER PALETTE

Fuchsia mulberry paper

Lime Green mulberry paper

Orange mulberry paper

Teal mulberry paper

✂ ABOUT THE PAPERS

Tissue-weight mulberry papers work well for this project because they fold easily and lay nicely on the canvas boards. The spray adhesive bonds to the paper and holds it firmly on the boards. Choose paper colors that coordinate with your child's room or with other home décor.

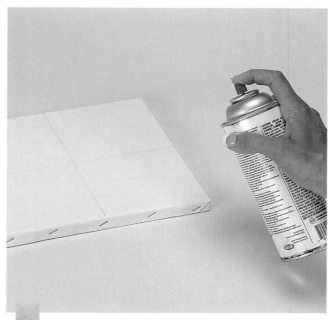

1 Rule Two Lines and Spray the Canvas

Lightly draw a horizontal and a vertical line in the center of each canvas. Spray a thin coat of adhesive to one of the canvases. Spray the sides as well. Let the adhesive dry until it is tacky.

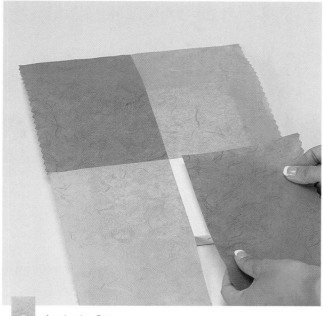

2 Apply the Papers

Trim two of each of the papers to 8½" × 5½" (22cm × 14cm). Lay two orange papers on opposite corners of the canvas. Be sure the paper corners and edges are aligned with the pencil lines. Smooth and press the paper onto the canvas and adhesive. Add the pink papers to the other corners.

3 Wrap the Paper Around the Edges

With the canvas face down, fold up the paper and crease it around to the back of the stretcher bar. Use double-stick tape to secure the paper to the stretcher bar. Fold in the corners like you would when wrapping a present.

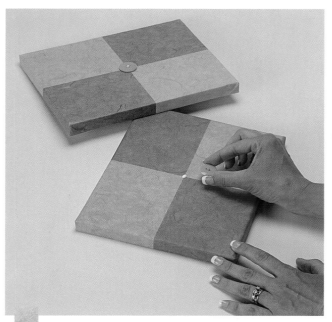

4 Add the Buttons

Repeat steps 1 through 3 for the other canvas and the blue and green paper. Thread a needle with embroidery floss and sew diagonally through the holes of one button to make a cross on the front. Use glue dots to adhere the button to the center of one canvas. Repeat for the other button and canvas.

Tic-Tac-Toe Table

What child doesn't like to play games? With its many shapes and colors, this game table may look complicated, but it's really quite simple to put together. With the durable glass-like finish, you won't have to worry if your little one uses it for a tea party as well.

MATERIALS

- small folding wooden table
- ⅝" (16mm) black paper ribbon
- découpage medium
- acrylic varnish
- Envirotex
- rotary cutter
- scissors
- various shapes template
- letters template
    or ShapeCutter and
    Letters-1, Fun Shapes-1,
    Circles-1, Squares-1
- cutting mat
- ruler
- tape measure
- ¾-inch (19mm) wash brush
- gloves
- disposable plastic sheet
- screwdriver
- wooden craft sticks
- two plastic cups

PAPER PALETTE

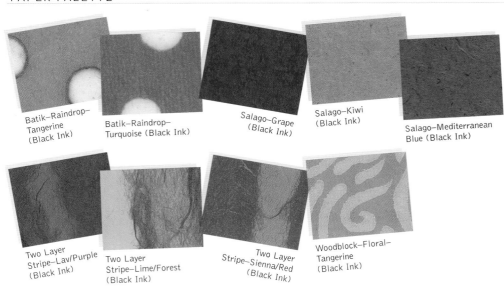

Batik–Raindrop–Tangerine (Black Ink)

Batik–Raindrop–Turquoise (Black Ink)

Salago–Grape (Black Ink)

Salago–Kiwi (Black Ink)

Salago–Mediterranean Blue (Black Ink)

Two Layer Stripe–Lav/Purple (Black Ink)

Two Layer Stripe–Lime/Forest (Black Ink)

Two Layer Stripe–Sienna/Red (Black Ink)

Woodblock–Floral–Tangerine (Black Ink)

✂ ABOUT THE PAPERS

I am just crazy about these polka dot papers! Batik is the technique used to make the dots. Wax is dropped onto handmade paper before it is dyed. Wherever the wax has been placed, the dye cannot be absorbed. You can actually feel the raised wax spots on the paper. This paper is made in Thailand.

1 Cut Out the Paper Pieces

Measure the width and length of your table and divide each of those measurements by three. This will be the measurement for one of nine rectangles. Use a rotary cutter and acrylic ruler to cut one rectangle from each of the nine assorted papers. You can stack the papers and cut all of them at the same time, if you wish. Lay the rectangles on the tabletop to see if they fit. Trim the papers to match the table if it has rounded corners. Using the chart on page 73, cut out shapes and letters with the ShapeCutter, templates and corresponding papers.

2 Add the Squares

The tabletop will be easier to work with if you remove its legs. Use a screwdriver to remove the legs and set the screws in a safe place so you can reassemble the table later. Apply the découpage medium to each corner of the table, add the paper rectangles and then cover the paper with more découpage medium.

X O X O

Paint wooden X's and O's with brightly colored acrylic paint, then seal them with acrylic varnish. Use them as game pieces for this great table or substitute any other objects.

3 Apply Remaining Pieces

Add the remaining rectangles to the tabletop using the same process, centering each piece accordingly.

4 Layer the Shapes and Letters

Découpage the letters forming words in a diagonal pattern across the tabletop. Add the shapes to the remaining rectangles. Without overworking the paper, cover the tabletop with another coat of découpage medium. Be sure to brush around all the shapes so the medium seals the edges of all the papers.

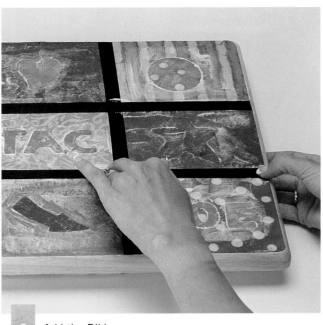

5 Add the Ribbon

Cut two pieces of black ribbon equal to the width of the tabletop and two pieces equal to the length of the tabletop. Lay the ribbon on the center of each of the paper seams to form a grid. Check your measurements with a ruler to insure your lines are straight and perpendicular to the edges. Cover the ribbon with découpage medium and allow everything to dry thoroughly.

3 Apply Varnish

Apply a coat of acrylic varnish on the entire tabletop surface. The varnish will prevent the Envirotex from seeping under the paper, so don't be tempted to skip this step. Be sure that all the edges of the paper shapes and the perimeter of the table are sealed. Let the varnish dry completely before moving to the next step.

7 Mix and Pour on the Clear Coat

Cover your work surface with a disposable plastic cloth. Follow the instructions on page 14 to mix the Envirotex. Pour the liquid over the tabletop.

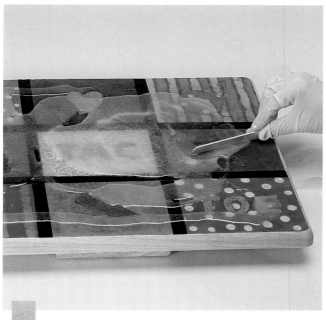

8 Spread the Mixture Over the Table

Use a craft stick to spread the liquid evenly over the table surface. Carefully move the liquid up to the edges without pushing it over the sides. If it does run over the sides, go ahead and spread it evenly on the sides and watch for drips as it dries. You can wipe away the drips with a craft stick.

9 Breathe Over the Bubbles and Set Aside

Soon you will see small bubbles forming in the clear coat. This is good! Wait five minutes for all the bubbles to rise to the surface. After five minutes has past, breathe warm air over the surface of the table as if you were trying to fog up a window. Watch the bubbles disappear before your eyes. The table will need about thirty-six hours to cure completely. Set it in a space where it can cure without being disturbed.

ShapeCutter Shapes

Kiwi	tic, tac, toe letters, and one heart
Batik-Turquoise	one 2" (5cm) square
Batik-Tangerine	one 2" (5cm) circle
Woodblock-Tangerine	one swirl
Grape	one arrow
Mediterranean Blue	one star

Striped Chair

When I found this inexpensive folding chair I knew it was the perfect companion for the Tic-Tac-Toe Table. It is very portable and can be easily folded up and put away. The slats in the seat make a perfect palette for the bright papers.

MATERIALS

- wooden folding chair
- découpage medium
- scissors
- rotary cutter
- cutting mat
- acrylic ruler
- tape measure
- pencil
- ¾-inch (19mm) wash brush

PAPER PALETTE

Batik–Raindrop–Turquoise (Black Ink)

Batik–Raindrop–Tangerine (Black Ink)

Two Layer Stripe–Lav/Purple (Black Ink)

Two Layer Stripe–Lime/Forest (Black Ink)

Two Layer Stripe–Sienna/Red (Black Ink)

Woodblock–Floral–Tangerine (Black Ink)

✂ ABOUT THE PAPERS

The floral design on the tangerine paper is stamped on the paper by hand using a wood block. This paper is made in India.

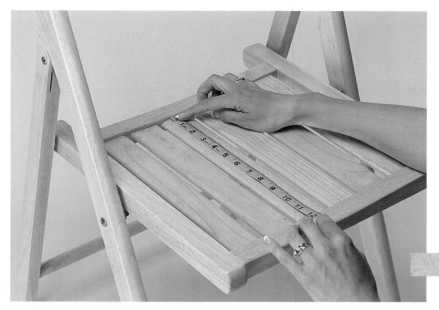

1 Measure Slat Length

Measure the length of the seat slats from the front of the chair to the back.

2 Measure Perimeter

Wrap the tape measure around one of the slats. Add ¼" (6mm) to this measurement to determine the width of the paper.

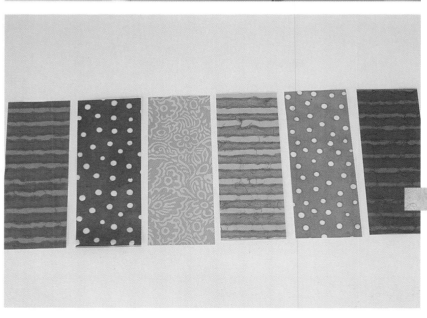

3 Cut Strips for the Seat

Use the measurements from steps 1 and 2 to determine the length and width of the paper. The pieces for this chair were 4½" × 12" (11cm × 30cm). Use the rotary cutter and acrylic ruler to cut out the papers for the seat. Arrange the papers on your work surface in the order they will be applied to the chair.

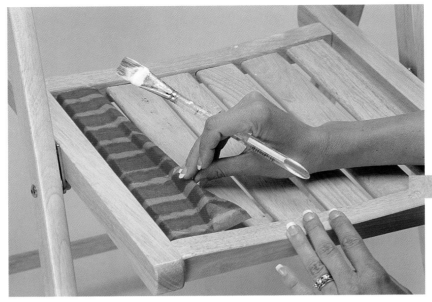

4 **Adhere the Seat Papers**

Use the wash brush to apply découpage medium to the top and bottom of one seat slat. Lay the first strip of paper on the slat and wrap the edges around the slat so the overlapped seam is on the underneath side of the seat. Coat the paper with more découpage medium. Repeat this step for the other seat slats.

5 **Add the Seat Trim**

Measure the length and width of the seat frame. Cut three pieces of paper 1" (3cm) × the width measurement and two pieces of paper 1" (3cm) × the length measurement. The length measurement should include wrapping the paper around the front and back edges. Use scissors to cut each strip into a wavy line. To save time, you can fold the long strips into quarters and cut the wavy line through all the layers at the same time. Adhere the side and front trims to the chair with découpage medium.

6 **Add the Rest of the Trim**

Adhere the last two paper strips to the top front and back of the chair. Coat all the trim pieces with a second layer of découpage medium.

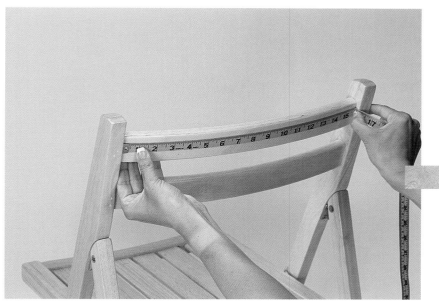

7 Measure the Back-Support Pieces

Wrap the tape measure around one of the back-support pieces and add ¼" (6mm) to the measurement for overlap. Measure the width of the back-support from the back of the chair. Divide this second measurement by six (because there are six seat slats and six different papers). You now have the length and width of the papers that will cover the chair back.

8 Trim Paper Into Strips

Cut two pieces from each paper that are the size configured from step 7. Here the pieces are 2⅝" × 5¼" (7cm × 13cm). Arrange the papers on your work surface in the order they will be applied to the chair.

9 Apply the First Row of Papers

Start on one side of the chair and begin coating both slats with découpage medium, using the ¾-inch (19mm) wash brush. Coat the front and the back. Apply the first piece of paper, starting it at the bottom of the slat and wrapping it all the way around. Repeat with the piece of paper on the lower slat.

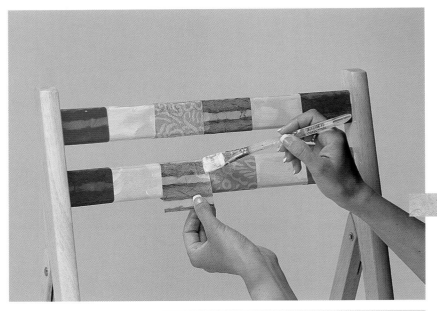

10 Find the Center

Adhere the two papers on the opposite end of the slats in the same manner. Mark the center point of the back of the chair slats with a pencil. Add the strips that go on either side of the center mark, using more découpage medium. The papers should overlap about ⅛" (3mm) at the center.

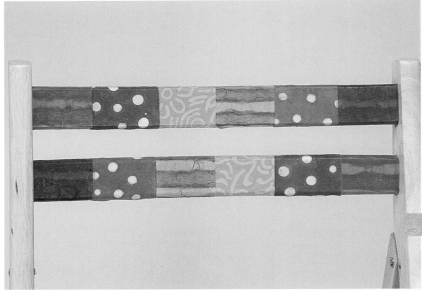

FIBER SOFTENER
For papers that are stiff and more difficult to wrap around a surface, it helps to brush découpage medium directly on the paper. The paper will become more pliable as the medium soaks into the paper.

11 Adhere the Remaining Strips of Paper

Apply the last four paper strips to the back of the chair. Trim the width of the papers if they overlap more than ⅛" (3mm) on both sides. Coat all the rows with a second layer of découpage medium.

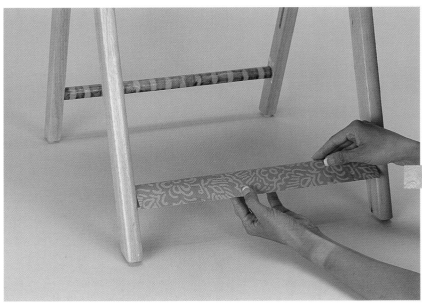

12 Apply Paper to the Rungs

Measure the rungs at the bottom of the chair, noting the width and the circumference, and add an extra ¼" (6mm) to the circumference. Cut two pieces of paper to this size. The size here is 3⅜" × 15½" (9cm × 39cm). Adhere these strips to the rungs with découpage medium and the wash brush. Give all of the paper surfaces a second coat of découpage medium to finish.

Mini Blue Chair

This miniature chair is decorated with blue and gold paper, using the same techniques as the slatted chair. The papers used here give the chair a little bit of Asian flair. This chair could be used to hold a china doll or hung on a wall and used for a shelf. It could also be used in other rooms of your home to hold a small glass votive and candle.

House Clock

Tick...tock...tick...tock. It only takes a few minutes to make this charming house clock. Simply cut out the shapes, découpage them to the papier-mâché form, add a clock component and in no time you are finished. You better get started, time is wasting!

MATERIALS

- papier-mâché house form
- clock component
- peel and stick numbers
- small wooden plug (for door knob)
- black permanent marker
- découpage medium
- gloss varnish
- craft glue
- scissors
- utility knife
- ShapeCutter or scissors
- large circle templates
- cutting mat
- pencil
- ¾-inch (19mm) wash brush
- drill
- wood shims
- patterns from page 122

PAPER PALETTE

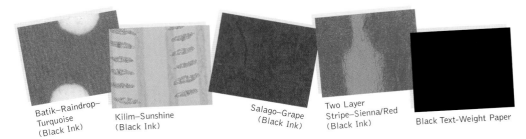

Batik–Raindrop–Turquoise (Black Ink)

Kilim–Sunshine (Black Ink)

Salago–Grape (Black Ink)

Two Layer Stripe–Sienna/Red (Black Ink)

Black Text-Weight Paper

✂ ABOUT THE PAPERS

Here is a mixture of batik, two layer, and woodblock papers. When I was growing up, it was a "fashion violation" to mix stripes with polka dots. Well. . .with this paper combination all the "rules" have been broken. Feel free to mix textures, colors and patterns.

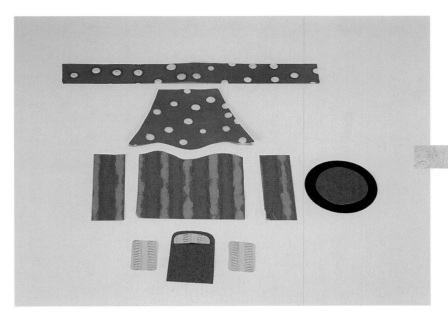

1 Cut Out the Shapes

Cut a 2½" (6cm) Grape circle and a 3½" (9cm) black circle with the ShapeCutter. Cut a strip from the Turquoise paper that is 1½" × 13¼" (4cm × 34cm). Cut two strips from the Sienna/ Red paper that are 1½" × 4½" (4cm × 11cm). Using the templates provided on page 122, cut a door from the Grape paper, two side windows and the door window from the Sunshine paper, the roof front from the Turquoise paper, and the house front from the Sienna/Red paper.

2 Trace the Clock Element

Lay the clock component on the back of the house form, 1½" (4cm) below the top of the house and trace it with a pencil.

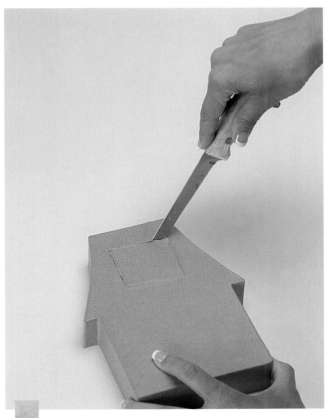

3 Create an Access Door

Cut three sides of the traced box to create an access door for the clock component, using the utility knife. Pull the three-sided flap out and make a crease on the fourth side.

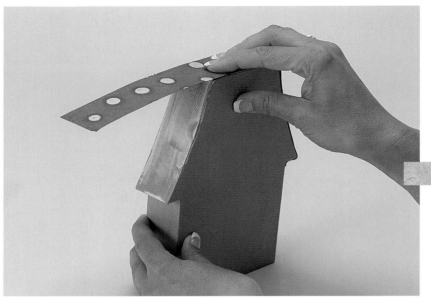

4 Adhere the Roof Top

Mark the center of the top of the roof with a pencil. Brush découpage medium over the top and sides of the roof using the wash brush. Fold the Turquoise strip in half to find the center and place this fold at the top center mark of the roof. Smooth the paper down the roof sides and tuck the paper under the eaves. Trim the excess paper if needed.

5 Add the House Sides

Coat the sides of the house with découpage medium and adhere the Sienna/Red paper strips to the house. Smooth out any wrinkles and wrap the excess paper around to the bottom of the house.

6 Add the House Front

Brush the front of the house with découpage medium and apply the front piece of striped paper.

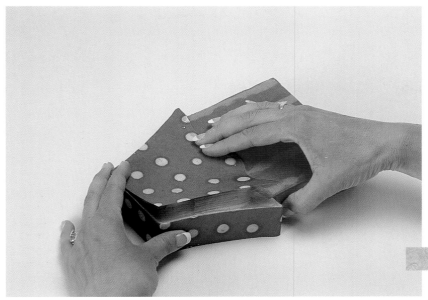

IT'S ABOUT TIME

Woodworking stores usually sell clock components separately, making it easy for you to choose the case, movement and hands that best suit your project. If you don't have a woodworking store nearby, the internet offers individual parts from several companies as well.

7 Add the Roof Front

Adhere the roof front to the house form. The roof should overlap the house front piece slightly.

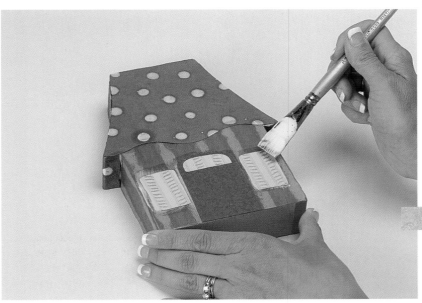

8 Adhere Door and Windows

Adhere the door to the center of the house. Align the bottom of the door with the bottom of the house. Adhere one window to the top of the door and the other two windows on each side of the door.

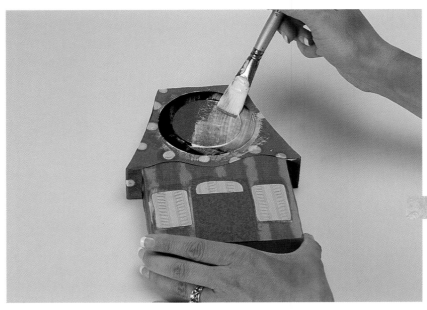

9 Add the Clock Circles

Place the black circle in the center of the roof and cover with découpage medium. Place the Grape circle in the center of the black circle and brush it with more medium. Cover the entire surface of the house with a generous coat of découpage medium. Let the house dry.

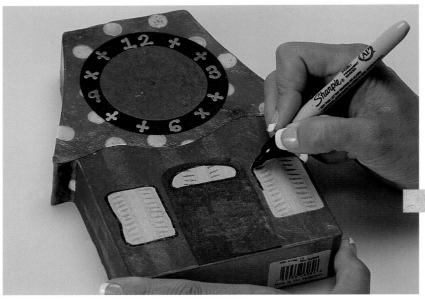

10 Outline the Details

Add the numbers to the clock using the scrap paper method shown for the cigar box clock (see step 8, page 37). Use a permanent black marker to outline all the paper shapes including the door, windows, roof line and all the edges of the house form.

11 Apply Gloss Varnish

Color the wooden plug with the permanent marker and glue it to the right side of the door. Apply a coat of gloss varnish to the entire house. When the varnish is dry, apply a second coat and let that dry completely.

12 Add the Clock Component

Mark the center of the Grape circle with a pencil and drill a hole large enough to accommodate the clock shaft. Place the clock component inside the back of the house through the access door. Follow the manufacturer's instructions to assemble the clock. If needed, add small wood or cardboard shims inside the house to accommodate the length of the clock shaft.

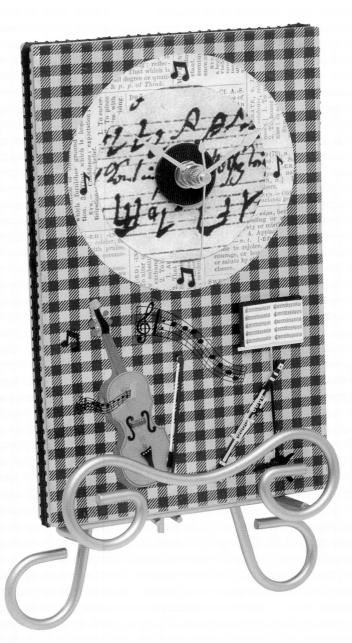

Music Clock

The base for this variation is a papier-maché rectangle instead of a house but the techniques are the same. The theme for this clock is music and the embellishments are 3-D stickers that I found in the scrapbooking section of a craft store. To make the music clock, cut out one paper rectangle and two circles and apply them to the papier maché base with decoupage medium. Attach the clock in the same manor as described in the house clock instructions. Use music notes for the clock numbers and add a piece of ribbon around the outside of the clock base. Display the clock on a beautiful plate stand.

office space

More and more people are working at home because of the technological advances in our information systems.

Home offices are popular but are often overlooked when it comes to decorating. An office must be functional but it can also be aesthetically pleasing. The container industry is exploding and that makes it easy for us to find organizational boxes and tubs for all of our stuff. However, some of them are not very attractive. In this chapter I will share project ideas that will add organization, function and decoration to your office space. Start by choosing a theme that you enjoy, find papers that match that theme and then just follow the directions!

Vintage Postcard File Box

I like this file box because it is sturdy and can be used to hold the files that need your immediate attention. Get those stacks of files off your desk and into the box. The vintage postcards add a decorative touch and can enhance or start a travel theme in your office.

MATERIALS

- cardboard file caddy (Highsmith)
- computer-generated file label
- metal label holder
- liquid laminate
- clear tape
- craft or wood glue
- deckle-edged scissors
- tape measure
- pencil
- ¾-inch (19mm) wash brush
- scrap cardboard
- drill
- plastic cup

PAPER PALETTE

Postcard scrapbook paper (K&Company)

Dark Green mulberry paper

ABOUT THE PAPERS

These paper postcards were cut out of scrapbook paper. For another option, look for old postcards in antique stores. I found several while I was "browsing" in an antique shop in Virginia this summer.

1 Cover Box Edges with Tape

Assemble the file box. Cover all the rough open edges of the box with clear tape. Cover the handle portion with tape so the opening is sealed.

2 Tear Mulberry Paper

Tear the entire sheet of green mulberry paper into random sizes and shapes. Remove all the straight edges from the paper pieces.

3 Adhere Paper to the Box

Brush an area of the box with liquid laminate. Lay a piece of paper over the laminated area. Saturate the paper with laminate using the ¾-inch (19mm) wash brush. Place the next piece of paper so it slightly overlaps the first paper on one side. Cover it with laminate. Repeat this until the entire box is covered with paper. Tear smaller pieces of paper as needed to fit in small spaces. Your box will look nicer if you wrap the paper over the edges of the box, rather than go up to the edge and stop.

4 Add Postcard Images

Cut out about ten paper postcard images with the deckle scissors. Randomly place the postcards over the outside of the file box using the same process that was used to apply the mulberry paper. Smooth any wrinkles away with your finger.

5 Support the Box to Dry

After all of the postcard images are laminated to the box, stuff the box with a couple of pieces of bent cardboard to keep the box from bowing while it dries. Let the box dry completely.

6 Mark the Front Center

Find the center front of the file box with a tape measure and mark it lightly with a pencil.

7 Drill Two Holes

Position the metal label holder over the center mark. Mark where the label holes are by punching the cardboard with a sharp pencil. Drill two holes into the box at the punch points.

8 Add the Label Holder

Squeeze a small amount of craft glue into the drilled holes. Position the label holder in place and drop the brads into the holes. Measure the label holder and create a paper file label to fit.

Travel Paper File Folders

To make coordinating file folders, apply double-stick adhesive sheets to the outside of the file folders. Adhere decorative paper to the file and turn under excess paper or trim it to fit the folder.

Stamp Box

For a coordinating storage box, decorate a paper box with stamps. There are scrapbook papers available with a stamp theme, or you could use actual stamps.

Travel Map Bulletin Board

Every office needs a bulletin board so why not make it attractive and unique? The map paper makes the bulletin board a nice complement to the other travel projects in this chapter. A few travel accessories like this project can give your office a pulled-together, polished look.

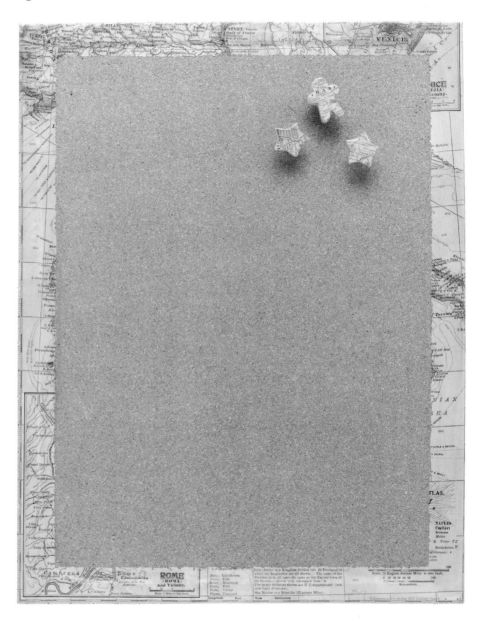

MATERIALS

- 17" × 23" (43cm × 58cm) cork board
- brown acrylic paint
- liquid laminate
- scissors
- deckle-edged scissors
- large acrylic ruler
- pencil
- ¾-inch (19mm) wash brush
- staple gun
- plastic cup

PAPER PALETTE

Actual Map or
28" × 20" (71cm × 51cm)
gift wrap

✂ ABOUT THE PAPERS

The map paper shown here is a piece of gift wrap, however, you can use any map that you find interesting. Choose a map of your city, a favorite vacation destination or a nautical map of a large body of water. If you want to antique the map, simply wipe it with antiquing gel or watered-down acrylic paint. If you are anxious to get your project started, use a blow dryer to speed the drying process.

1 Trim the Map

Center the corkboard over three sides of the back of the map paper. Trim the excess paper off of the top, leaving the same width as there is on the other three sides.

2 Measure for Inside Cut

Use the acrylic ruler to mark the paper for the inside cut. Measure in 2½" (6cm) on all sides of the paper and draw a light pencil line.

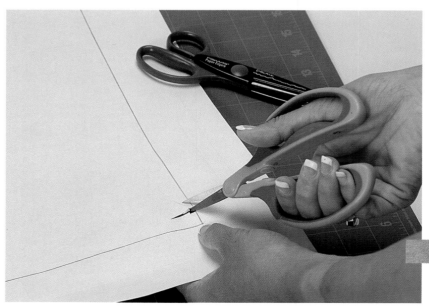

3 Create an Entry Hole

Make a small hole with a craft knife or scissors on the inside of the pencil line. Expand the hole so it is large enough for the deckle scissors to fit.

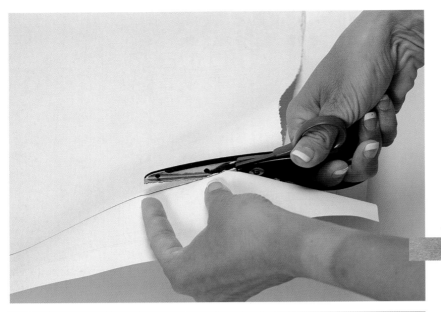

4   Remove Center Paper Piece

Cut around the pencil line with the deckle scissors. Remove the center piece and set it aside for another project.

LEFTOVERS?
Any extra paper from this project can be used for either the file folders on page 91 or the pushpins on page 97.

5   Fold the Paper over the Sides

Center the board over the back of the deckle-cut paper. Fold and crease each side of the paper over the back of the board.

6   Staple the Paper

Staple the paper to one short side of the board with about three staples. Leave about 4" (10cm) from each corner unstapled. Repeat this on the other short side of the board. Place one staple in the center of each long side.

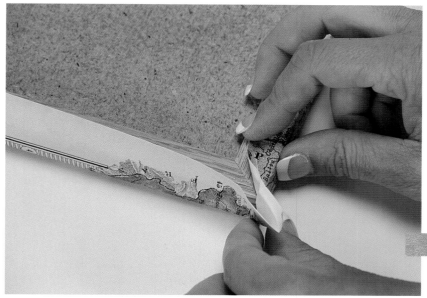

7 **Fold the Corners**

Bring both sides of the paper together at the corner and pinch the paper to create a nice, sharp crease.

8 **Fold and Crease**

Fold the point to one side of the board and crease the paper at the corner.

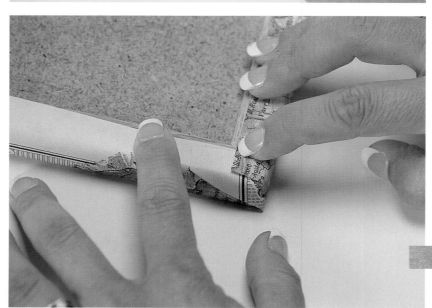

9 **Fold Excess Paper**

Fold the paper that is left above the board toward the center of the board. Press and fold to make a sharp crease.

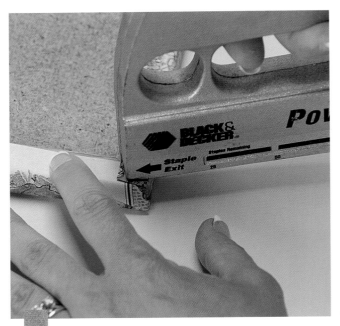

10 Staple the Corner

Place a staple in the corner to hold the fold. Repeat this process for the other three corners. Add additional staples to the long and short sides of the board spacing them about 2½" (6cm) apart.

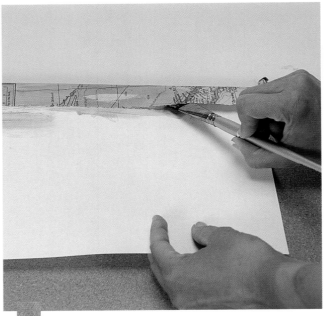

11 Apply Tinted Medium to Paper

Pour some liquid laminate into a cup and add about three drops of brown acrylic paint. Stir the laminate to mix the paint. Add more drops of paint if you want a darker antique color. Turn the board right side facing up. Slide a piece of paper under the edge of the map paper to protect the corkboard. Apply laminate to the underneath side of the map paper. Cover the front side of the map paper with laminate.

12 Smooth the Paper Over the Sides

Use your fingers to press down and smooth the paper over the side of the corkboard frame. Continue to work in small areas around the frame. Add additional laminate to make paper more pliable. Smooth the paper so it is firmly bonded to the board.

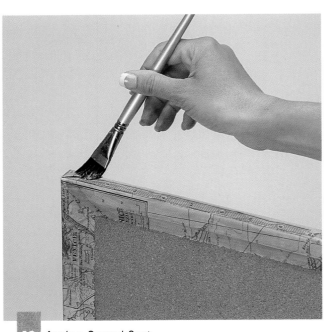

13 Apply a Second Coat

Brush the tinted laminate over the paper on the sides and back of the frame to coat the entire paper surface. Let dry. Apply one more coat of laminate.

Pushpins

Here is a good way to use up extra scrapbook papers or small pieces of gift wrap. These pushpins are fun to create and make an excellent gift for friends and family members of all ages. Make several sets and have them on hand for those last-minute hostess or teacher gifts.

MATERIALS

- wood shapes, ½" (12mm) thick
- pushpins
- small scraps of map
- découpage medium
- Envirotex
- craft glue
- no. 10 shader brush
- small piece of ¼" (6mm) cardboard
- gloves
- wooden craft stick
- two plastic cups

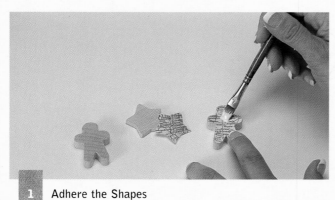

1 Adhere the Shapes

Trace the shapes onto the back of the map paper, cut out the shapes and apply découpage medium to the wood shapes with the brush. Place the paper shapes onto the wood shapes and cover with a coat of découpage medium. Be sure the paper edges are firmly bonded to the wood. Let dry, apply a second coat of medium, and let dry again.

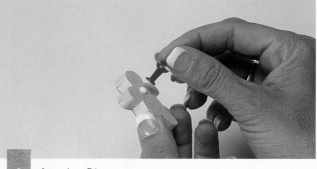

2 Attach a Pin

Glue a pushpin to the back of each wood shape, using craft glue.

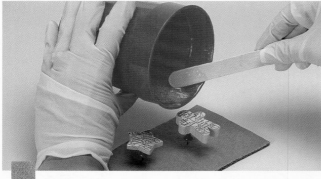

3 Prepare Clear Coat

Stick the pins into the piece of cardboard. Prepare a small batch of Envirotex (see page 14–15) and pour over the shapes.

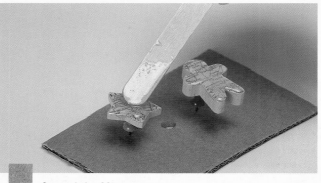

4 Spread the Mixture

Spread the mixture over the shapes evenly with a craft stick. Set aside to cure.

Travel Map Storage Box

Use this chic container to store your tape, stapler, scissors or loose photos. The wooden feet add a trendy look and change an ordinary box into something special. Shop around for a distinctive knob for the top of the box. There are many different shapes and themes available.

MATERIALS

- storage box (Highsmith)
- wooden mushroom knobs, 4
- black metal drawer knob
- ½" (12mm) screw that fits knob
- washer
- black acrylic paint
- brown acrylic paint
- liquid laminate
- craft glue
- acrylic ruler
- no. 10 shader brush
- ¾-inch (19mm) wash brush
- pencil
- drill
- plastic cup

PAPER PALETTE

London Map scrapbook paper (K&Company)

✂ ABOUT THE PAPERS

Scrapbook paper is available in 12" × 12" (30cm × 30cm) and 8½" × 11" (22cm × 28cm) pieces. These are good sizes for small projects like the map box. Look for vintage map paper or other travel-themed papers.

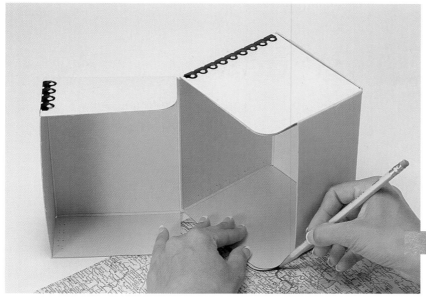

1 Trace the Box

Place the map paper right side up and set one side of the box on the paper. Trace the perimeter of that side of the box.

2 Tear the Paper

Tear the paper inside of the pencil lines. Hold down the side that is to be used, and with your other hand, tear toward you. This will create a white deckle edge on the paper that will soak up the antique color of the laminate. Repeat this step until you have a piece of torn paper for all sides of the box. Adjust the size of the paper pieces as needed to fit the sides of the box and label the back of each piece, e.g. top, back, left upper and so on.

3 Add Tint to the Liquid Laminate

Pour some liquid laminate into the plastic cup and add about three drops of brown acrylic paint. Stir the laminate to mix the paint. Add more paint if you want a darker antique tint.

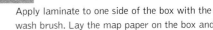

4 Adhere Map Pieces to the Box

Apply laminate to one side of the box with the wash brush. Lay the map paper on the box and brush it with laminate starting in the middle of the paper and working to the edges. Smooth out any wrinkles that appear with your finger. Continue adding paper to all sides of the box. Let dry.

5 Paint the Wooden Knobs

Paint four mushroom knobs with black acrylic paint. Use the no. 10 shader brush. Set the knobs aside to dry. When they are dry, brush each knob with a coat of laminate.

6 Mark the Spot for the Metal Knob

Use an acrylic ruler and a pencil to mark the center of the box lid. Lay the ruler diagonally from one corner to the other and draw a small pencil line in the center. Then, lay the ruler diagonally across the other corners and draw a small line in the center. The two lines will form an X.

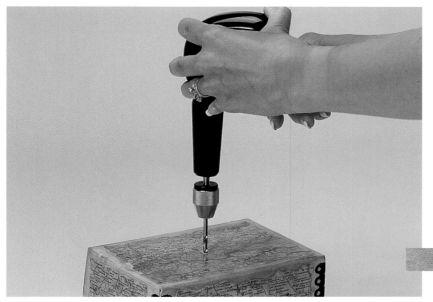

7   Drill a Hole

Drill a hole in the center of the X. Attach the knob with a screw and washer.

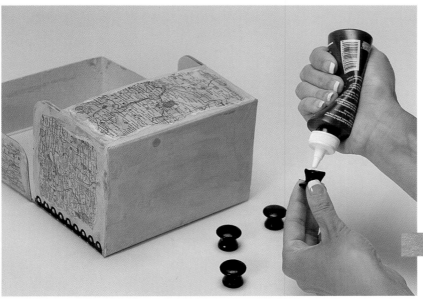

8   Add Glue to the Knobs

After the painted knobs have dried, apply a coat of liquid laminate to each. When they are dry, begin applying craft glue to the end of each knob.

9   Add the Knobs to the Box

Adhere one knob to each of the four bottom corners of the box.

Asian Magazine Holder

The beautiful Asian papers inspired this project. The combination of the red, gold and black make a bold statement. The added dimension of the Chinese coins and the metal file label give it a professional finish.

MATERIALS

- cardboard magazine holder (Highsmith)
- computer-generated label
- metal label holder
- Chinese coins, 8
- liquid laminate
- paper glaze
- craft glue
- clear tape
- scissors
    or ShapeCutter and Large Rectangles, Rectangles-1
- cutting mat
- tape measure
- ¾-inch (19mm) wash brush
- pencil
- rubber band
- drill
- plastic cup
- craft paint bottle

PAPER PALETTE

Black/Gold Stripe Silkscreen (Black Ink)

Chinese Letter–Gold/Red (Black Ink)

Hanja Script–Gold on Red (Black Ink)

✂ ABOUT THE PAPERS

Hanja script is a beautiful paper that has small gold Chinese text. The writing is from a bible of morality by Confucius. The fiber content is Kozo, and it is machine made. The diamond Chinese letter paper is made from mulberry and bamboo, and the letters say "good luck."

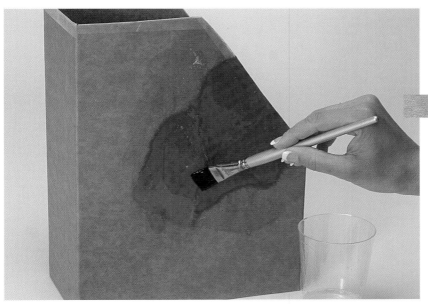

1 Assemble and Cover the Box

Assemble the magazine box. Cover all the raw edges of the box with clear tape. Tear the small script paper into random shapes, but similar-sized pieces. Remove all the straight edges from the paper pieces. Brush an area of the box with liquid laminate. Lay a piece of paper over the laminated area. Saturate the paper with laminate using the ¾-inch (19mm) wash brush. Place the next piece of paper so it slightly overlaps the first paper. Cover it with laminate. Repeat this until the entire box is covered with paper. Tear smaller pieces of paper as needed to fit in small spaces. Set the box aside.

WELL-ROUNDED

When covering a surface with the initial layer of paper, your box will look nicer if you wrap the paper over the edges of the box, rather than go up to the edge and stop.

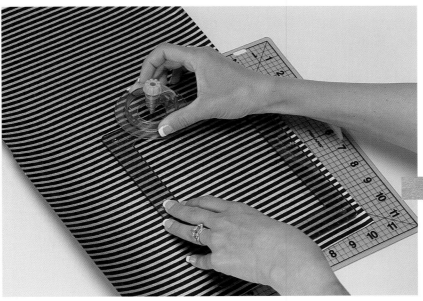

2 Cut out the Paper Embellishments

Cut out the following pieces of paper using the ShapeCutter and templates. Cut out two 9" × 7" (23cm × 18cm) gold striped rectangles; cut out two 8" × 6" (20cm × 15cm) Chinese Letter rectangles; cut out one 5" × 3" (13cm × 8cm) gold striped rectangle and one 4" × 2½" (10cm × 6cm) Chinese Letter rectangle.

3 Fold the Corner and Trim

Lay one of the large striped papers on the side of the box. Center it so that the sides have even spacing and the bottom edge is about ¼" (6mm) from the bottom edge of the box. Fold one corner of the paper down to match the angle of the box. Fold it down far enough to match the spacing at the sides of the box. Crease the paper at the fold line. Align both large striped papers with backsides together. Trim away the corner at the fold line. Repeat this step for the Chinese Letter papers centering it on the gold striped paper.

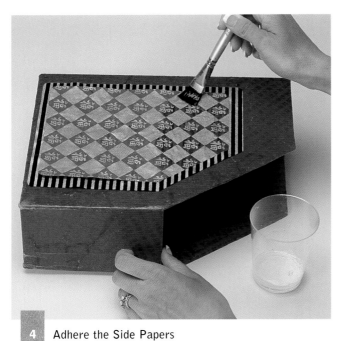

4 Adhere the Side Papers

Adhere one large gold stripe and one Chinese Letter to each side of the box. Wet the side of the box with laminate and then layer the papers adding laminate between each layer.

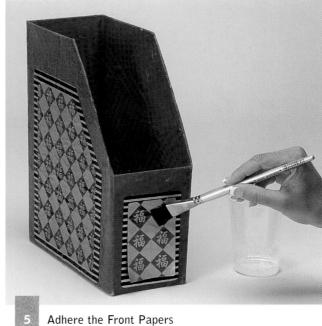

5 Adhere the Front Papers

Use scissors to trim ½" (12mm) off the smallest gold stripe paper so it measures 4½" × 3" (11cm × 8cm). Adhere that paper to the front of the box. Center the paper from side to side and match the bottom edge of the paper with the side pieces of the same color. Adhere the small Chinese Letter paper to the front of the gold stripe paper.

6 Stage the Box for Drying

Set a craft paint bottle at the top front corners of the box. Wrap a rubber band around the top of the box and in front of the paint bottle. This will hold the shape of the box while it is drying. Let dry completely.

7 Apply Paper Glaze

Cover the entire surface of the magazine holder with paper glaze. Use the ¾-inch (19mm) wash brush to apply the glaze. Let dry.

8 Add the Coin Embellishments

Glue four coins to each side of the holder. Center the coins in the open space above the striped paper.

9 Add the Label Holder

Find the center front of the magazine holder with a tape measure and mark it lightly with a pencil. Position the metal label holder over the center mark. Mark the label holes by punching the cardboard with a sharp pencil. Drill two holes into the box at the punch points. Squeeze a small amount of craft glue into the drilled holes. Position the label holder in place and drop the brads into the holes. Print a label on your computer and cut it to fit in the metal holder.

Asian Storage Tote

This tote is made the same way as the magazine holder. The accents are made by taking strips of paper and punching a decorative design along both edges. The same punch was used to make the black square.

Far East Mouse Pad

Are you tired of your boring old mouse pad? Here is a project that will transform an ordinary mouse pad into something that will jazz up your desk. Any shape or size will do, but I prefer a fairly square shape for this particular design.

MATERIALS

- standard mouse pad
- découpage medium
- scissors
- 6" (15cm) circle template
- 3" (8cm) circle template or ShapeCutter and Large Circles, Circles-1
- cutting mat
- pencil
- ¾-inch (19mm) wash brush
- plastic cup
- craft paint bottles or paper weights

PAPER PALETTE

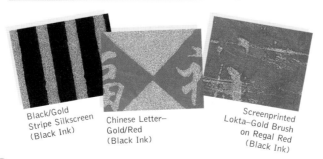

Black/Gold Stripe Silkscreen (Black Ink)

Chinese Letter– Gold/Red (Black Ink)

Screenprinted Lokta–Gold Brush on Regal Red (Black Ink)

ABOUT THE PAPERS

Lotka is a bush that grows in the Himalayan Mountains of Nepal. The bush can regenerate itself in about four years making it an environmentally friendly paper resource. These papers are handmade and vegetable dyed.

1 Cut out the Papers

Turn the Screenprinted paper upside down and trace around the mouse pad lightly with a pencil. Cut this shape out with scissors. Use the ShapeCutter and templates to cut out shapes from the following paper pieces: one 5½" (14cm) square and one 3" (8cm) circle from the gold striped paper, and one 6" (15cm) circle from the Chinese Letter paper.

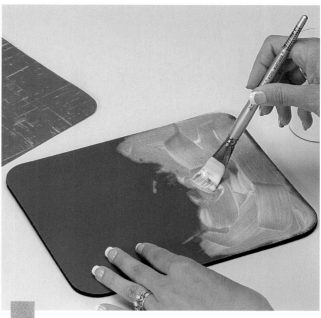

2 Apply Découpage Medium

Cover the front of the mouse pad with découpage medium. Apply two coats if a lot of the medium soaks into the pad too quickly.

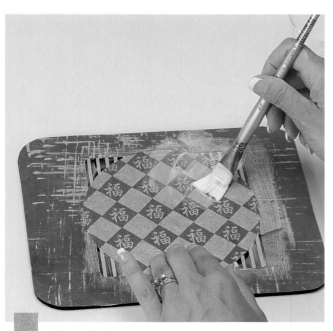

3 Adhere the Paper

Lay the Screenprinted paper shape on top of the mouse pad. Smooth it onto the mouse pad with your hands starting in the center and working toward the edges. Cover this paper with découpage medium. Layer the other papers in the center of the mouse pad adding découpage medium between each layer.

4 Apply a Second Coat

Apply a second coat of découpage medium over the surface of the mouse pad. Let it dry. Weight each corner of the mouse pad with a craft paint bottle if the corners begin to curl.

family space

The family room is truly the heart of the home. As such, it should reflect a balance of everyone's traits and personalities, emphasizing fun over fussy! More so than in any other room, this is your opportunity to relax and create a space where everyone can be themselves.

In this chapter you will learn how to make several accessories for your family's favorite space. The projects are kid friendly, easy to make and a bit whimsical. The brightly colored Lantern String, for instance, keeps the magic of holiday lights in your surroundings all year-round, while the Game Lampshade may just be the inspiration to corral everyone together regularly for Family Game Night.

Lantern String

These paper lanterns can be hung just about anywhere. They add a fun ambience to a room when all the other lights are turned out. As a variation, you can cut out letters that spell your family's name and adhere them to the lanterns instead of the stripes and geometric shapes.

MATERIALS

- paper lantern set
- string of lights
- découpage medium
- scissors
- 2" (5cm) and 1" (3cm) star templates
- 2" (5cm) and 1" (3cm) circle templates
- 2" (5cm) and 1" (3cm) square templates
- 3¼" × 1¾" (8cm × 4cm) diamond template
- 1¾" × 1" (4cm × 3cm) diamond template
  or ShapeCutter and Circles-1, Diamonds-1, Stars-1, Squares-1
- rotary cutter
- cutting mat
- acrylic ruler
- ¾-inch (19mm) wash brush

PAPER PALETTE

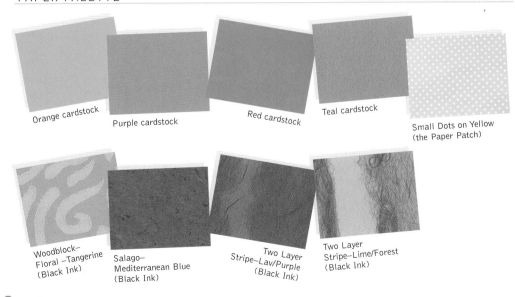

Orange cardstock

Purple cardstock

Red cardstock

Teal cardstock

Small Dots on Yellow (the Paper Patch)

Woodblock– Floral –Tangerine (Black Ink)

Salago– Mediterranean Blue (Black Ink)

Two Layer Stripe–Lav/Purple (Black Ink)

Two Layer Stripe–Lime/Forest (Black Ink)

✂ ABOUT THE PAPERS

The two layer stripe paper is made with a base of colored mulberry paper and then topped with a tissue weight Unryu of a different color. The stripes can only be seen on one side of the paper. Fiber strands add visual texture to the paper and yet the surface is fairly smooth. The print on the Tangerine mulberry paper is created using a hand-carved woodblock.

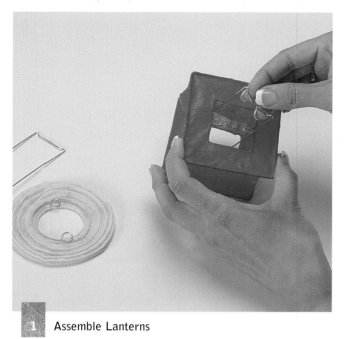

1 Assemble Lanterns

Pull the paper lanterns open and insert the wire supports.

2 Add Shapes to Cube Lanterns

Cut out the cardstock paper shapes with the ShapeCutter and the corresponding templates to make donut-shaped circles, squares, diamonds and stars (see Cutting a Donut Shape, page 12). Cut the inside shapes first, followed by the outside shapes. See the chart on page 122 for specifics on color and shape. Lay out the shapes with the corresponding square lanterns (see page 122 to match the shapes with the proper square lanterns). Begin adding the shapes to the lanterns, using découpage medium and the wash brush. Apply additional medium over the shapes.

3 Add Shapes to Ball Lanterns

Use the rotary cutter and acrylic ruler to cut strips of paper ⅜" × 4½" (10mm × 11cm) according to the chart on page 122. Lay out the paper strips with the corresponding round lanterns. Adhere the paper strips to the round lanterns using the same process as for the square lanterns. Tuck in the strip on either end. Let all of the lanterns dry.

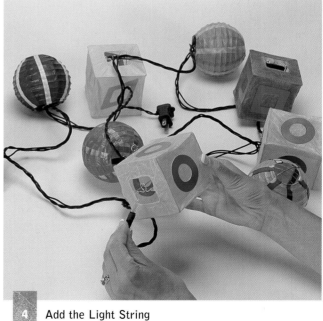

4 Add the Light String

Assemble the lanterns to the light string. Each light clips into the top of a lantern. Alternate the cubes and the balls.

Floating Frame

This is a unique picture frame because the framed items are floating between two pieces of glass. The design is a combination of different textures, metallic threads and faux metal tiles. The tiles look like they are three dimensional with embossed designs. There are many different tile designs so you can find one you like or, if you have a collection of coins or medallions, you can substitute those for the metal tiles.

MATERIALS

- 8" × 10" (20cm × 25cm) float frame
- faux metal tiles (Teapots and Clocks by Nancy Smith)
- metallic copper thread
- double-stick tape
- scissors
- ruler
- pencil
- ¾-inch (19mm) wash brush
- needle
- plastic cup
- water

PAPER PALETTE

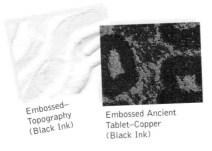

Embossed— Topography (Black Ink)

Embossed Ancient Tablet—Copper (Black Ink)

✂ ABOUT THE PAPERS

All three of these papers come from Thailand. Ancient Tablet features the Thai alphabet embossed in copper. The general meaning of the letters describes Sukhothai as the land of fertility, peace and morality.

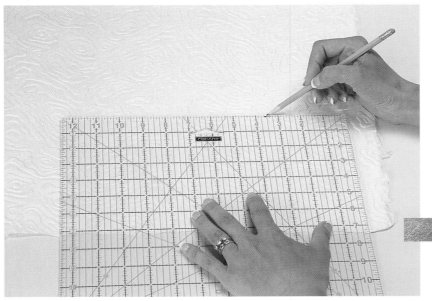

1 Measure and Mark Papers

Draw a 5½" × 7½" (14cm × 19cm) rectangle on the back of the embossed white paper and a 7" × 9" (18cm × 23cm) rectangle on the back of the Ancient Tablet paper.

2 Wet the Paper

Trace along the pencil lines with a water-filled brush. Create a water line about ¾" (19mm) wide.

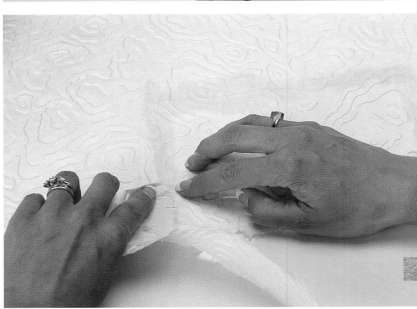

3 Tear the Paper

Gently tear along the pencil line to create a deckled edge.

4 Stitch the Paper

Thread the needle with three strands of metallic copper thread. Stitch the white paper to the Ancient Tablet paper with random stitches about ¾" (19mm) long and about ¾" (19mm) apart. Stitch all the way around the edges. Tie off the ends at the back of paper and cut off the excess thread. Apply double-stick tape to the metallic paper and adhere it to the back of the script paper to cover the stitches.

5 Cut Out Tiles

Cut out six faux metal tiles: two clocks and four teapots.

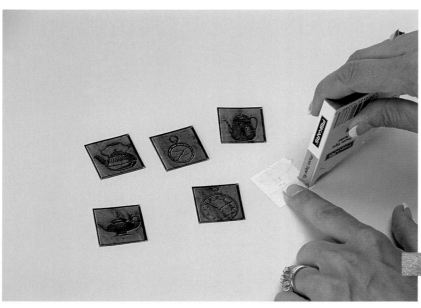

6 Apply Double-Stick Tape

Apply double-stick tape to the back of each tile and peel off the paper backing.

7 **Adhere the Tiles**

Adhere the tiles to the center of the white embossed paper in rows of three. Place the clock tiles in the center of each row.

8 **Remove Glass from the Frame**

Open the frame and remove the two panes of glass. Sandwich the paper between the glass.

9 **Replace the Glass**

Insert the glass panes back in the frame.

10 **Replace the Frame Casing**

Replace the frame casing and secure it with brads.

Punched Luminaries

These lanterns are fun because they illuminate the shapes that you punch into the paper. Place a votive inside the lanterns and see the light flow through the mulberry paper. I envision three to five of these together on a coffee table, a fireplace mantel or outside around a garden patio.

MATERIALS

- spray adhesive
- teal and red thread
- rotary cutter
- decorative long-necked punches
    - small circle
    - star
    - sun
    - swirl
- cutting mat
- ruler
- sewing machine
- protective surface for spraying

PAPER PALETTE

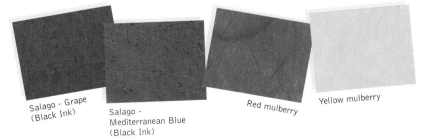

Salago - Grape
(Black Ink)

Salago -
Mediterranean Blue
(Black Ink)

Red mulberry

Yellow mulberry

✂ ABOUT THE PAPERS

Salago is a heavy weight paper and is a good contrast to the light weight mulberry paper. These lanterns work because the Salago gives body to the lantern while the mulberry paper allows the candle light to shine through.

1 Cut Paper and Punch Out Swirls

Cut four pieces each of red and grape papers to 5½" × 6" (14cm × 15cm). Trim three pieces each of the teal and yellow papers to 5½" × 11" (14cm × 28cm). Set the red and yellow papers aside. Randomly punch out swirls and stars from each piece of the teal and grape pieces. Keep punches at least ¾" (19mm) from the edges.

2 Adhere Red Paper

Spray the backs of each punched piece with spray adhesive. Place a piece of red paper over the sticky side of each Grape piece, and smooth it out with your hand. Repeat for the teal and yellow pieces.

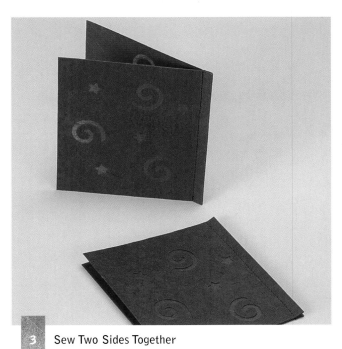

3 Sew Two Sides Together

Lay two pieces of the grape/red papers together with the red mulberry papers touching. Sew them together lengthwise with a sewing machine. The seam allowance is ¼" (6mm). Repeat this for the other two grape/red paper pieces.

4 Connect the Remaining Sides

Match the two unsewn edges of the papers together. Sew the papers together to form a complete square. Flatten out the seams to expose the red paper. Repeat steps 3 and 4 for the teal/yellow papers. Their three sides will form a tall triangle.

Game Lampshade

I can't think of a more appropriate
lamp for a family space than one that
is embellished with game pieces
and cards. You can create an entire
decorating theme around this one
lamp. Think of the possibilities. By
the way, do you have an eight?

MATERIALS

• lampshade
• thin cardboard
• poker chips
• wooden dominos
• burgundy cord trim
• double-sided adhesive sheet
• transparent tape
• craft glue
• deckle-edged scissors
• ¾-inch (19mm) wash brush
• spray can

PAPER PALETTE

Fortune Cards
scrapbook paper
(Design Originals)

Game Cards
scrapbook paper
(Design Originals)

Vintage Cards
scrapbook paper
(Design Originals)

Scrabble Letters
scrapbook paper

✂ ABOUT THE PAPERS

The playing card papers are new but have a vintage look and can be found in
the scrapbook section of most craft stores. I found three different patterns that
coordinated nicely and then added game pieces to the lamp for dimension.

1 Cut Out the Cards

Use the deckle-edged scissors to cut out card shapes from all three of the papers. Vary the amount of cards that you leave connected (cut some that are connected horizontally, some that are connected vertically, and some that are singles).

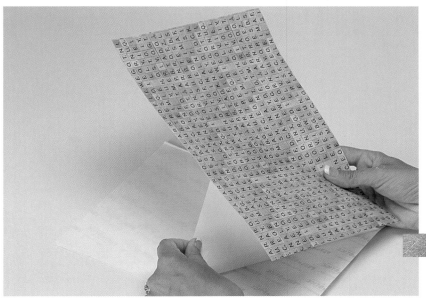

2 Add Dimension to Scrabble Paper

To give the Scrabble paper more dimension, mount it to a piece of cardboard with a sheet of double-sided adhesive and set it aside.

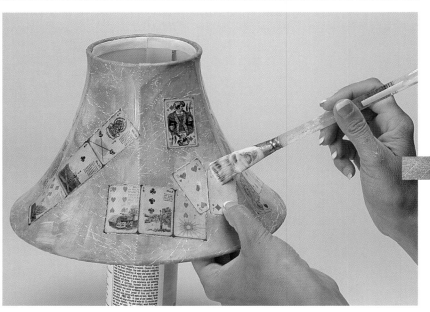

3 Apply Card Pieces to the Shade

Apply découpage medium to the outside of the lampshade, using the wash brush. Add the cut-out paper pieces in a random fashion and apply more medium over the top of the papers. Continue adding card pieces around the entire shade. Place the lampshade on top of a spray can when you are working on it. This will lift it off your work surface and allow you to spin the shade as you work.

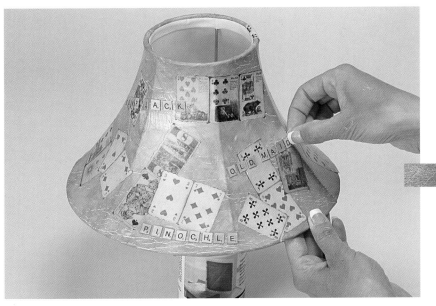

4 **Add Letters to the Shade**

Cut out Scrabble letters that spell card games. The words that I used are bridge, manipulation, rummy, go fish, canasta, old maid, kings, blackjack, pinochle, slapjack and hearts. Arrange the Scrabble letters in rows so you can see how much space the words will require. Use découpage medium to add the words randomly to the lampshade.

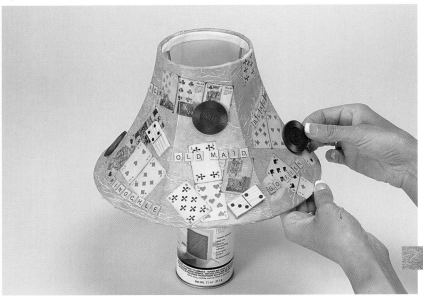

5 **Adhere the Game Pieces**

Add dominos and poker chips to the shade, adhering them with craft glue.

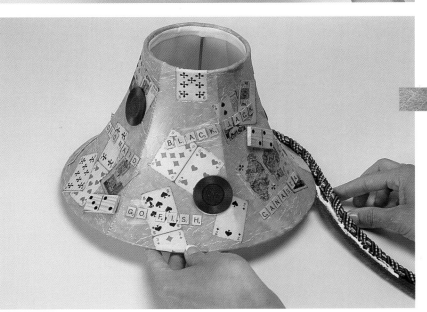

6 **Adhere Burgundy Trim to the Shade**

Lay the burgundy trim around the bottom of the shade and cut a piece that is about 4" (10cm) larger than the circumference. Cut a second piece of trim for the top of the shade, again leaving about 4" (10cm). If you place a piece of transparent tape around the trim before you cut it, it will prevent the trim from fraying. Apply glue to the portion of the trim that goes on the inside of the shade. Put the shade flat on your work surface. Lift one edge of the shade and slide the edge of the trim under the shade. Press the shade down on top of the trim to hold it in place while the glue dries. Continue lifting the shade and sliding the trim underneath.

7 Cut the Burgundy Trim

When the trim is all the way around the bottom of the shade, center a piece of tape around the trim at the spot you will want to cut it, and then cut the trim at the center of the tape. Place a bead of craft glue on the end of the trim. Press the two ends together to bond the raw edges. Remove the tape when the glue has dried completely.

8 Repeat for the Trim at the Top

Repeat the gluing process for the length of trim that goes around the top of the shade, starting it at the same seam as the bottom piece.

Newspaper Lamp

The only differences between the Game Lampshade and this one are the paper, embellishments and trim selection. The techniques for creating them are the same. The papers are all vintage newspaper advertisements and word definitions from the dictionary. The black letters are stickers that look like old typewriter keys. The letters spell words that relate to newspapers. The words that I used are tabloid, news, daily, ink, puzzle, paper, article, font and words. See how you can change the look of the project by the papers that you choose? Find papers that inspire you and then build on that theme.

Patterns and Tables

Lantern String page 110

Donut Shapes	Outside	Inside
Star (4 orange)	2" (5cm)	1" (3cm)
Circle (8 teal)	2" (5cm)	1" (3cm)
Square (4 red)	2" (5cm)	1" (3cm)
Diamond (4 purple)	$3\frac{1}{4}$" × $1\frac{3}{4}$" (8cm × 4cm)	$1\frac{3}{4}$" × 1" (4cm × 3cm)

Strips

Strips (6 of each color)) $\frac{3}{8}$" × $4\frac{1}{2}$" (10cm × 11cm)
Lav/Purple, Lime/Forest, Tangerine, Mediterranean Blue, Yellow Dot)

Lantern Color Order

Round: red with green strips
Square: lime green with teal circles
Round: orange with teal strips
Square: blue with red squares
Round: green with orange strips
Square: orange with purple diamonds
Round: dark blue with yellow strips
Square: red with orange stars
Round: yellow with purple strips
Square: lime green with teal circles

House Clock page 80

House Clock Templates
Use at 148%

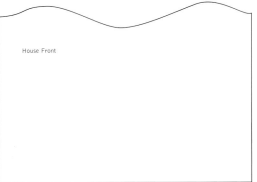

House Front

Door Window

Door

Window

Roof Front

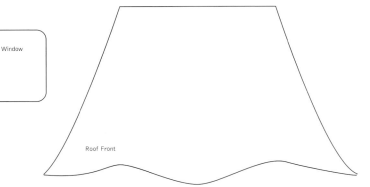

Decorative Screen page 42

Diagram 1, Layout of Papers

Side Panel(s)

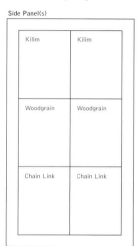

Kilim	Kilim
Woodgrain	Woodgrain
Chain Link	Chain Link

Center Panel

Kilim	Mango	Kilim
Woodgrain	Riviere	Woodgrain
Chain Link	Mango	Chain Link

Diagram 2, Measuring Side Panels

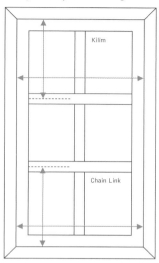

Kilim

Chain Link

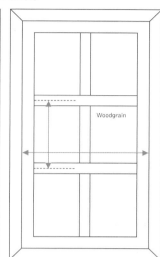

Woodgrain

Diagram 3, Measuring Center Panel

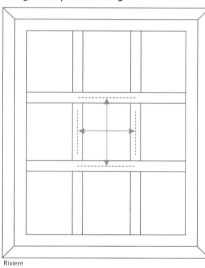

Riviere

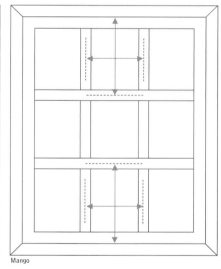

Mango

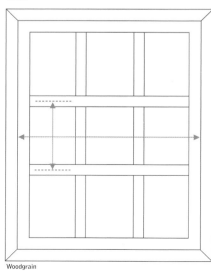

Woodgrain

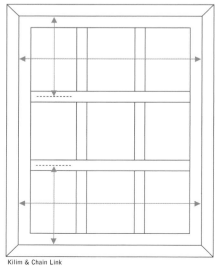

Kilim & Chain Link

Resources

All of the materials and paper used in this book should be easy to find at your local arts and crafts store, hardware store or specialty paper store. If, however, you have trouble locating any items, consult this list for information on where these manufacturers' products are distributed for retail.

Beacon Adhesives
125 S MacQuesten Parkway
Mount Vernon, NY 10550
(800) 865-7238
www.beaconcreates.com
Beacon's Liquid Laminate

Design Originals
2425 Cullen Street
Fort Worth, TX 76107
(800) 877-7820
www.d-originals.com
Scrapbook Papers

Environmental Technology, Inc. (ETI)
South Bay Depot Road
Fields Landing, CA 95537
(707) 443-9323
www.eti-usa.com
Envirotex Lite

Fiskars Brands, Inc.
7811 West Stewart Avenue
Wausau, WI 54401
www.fiskars.com
ShapeCutter
ShapeCutter Templates
Rotary Cutter
Cutting Mat
Hand Drill
Deckle Scissors
Acrylic Rulers

Gold Leaf Paper Company
P.O. Box 458
Brisbane, CA 94005
Kozo Paper

Graphic Products Corporation
455 Maple Avenue
Carpentersville, IL 60110
(800) 323-1660
www.gpcpapers.com
Black Ink Papers

Highsmith Inc.
W5527 State Road 106
Fort Atkinson, WI 53538
(800) 558-2110
www.highsmith.com
File Caddy (Q53-34722)
Kraft Magazine File (Q53-48930)
Table Totes (Q53-24345)
Negative and Print Envelope
Storage Boxes (Q53-24241)

K&Company
8500 N.W. River Park Drive
Pillar #136
Parkville, MO 64152
(888) 244-2083
www.kandcompany.com
Scrapbook Papers

Karen Foster Design
623 North 1250 West
Centerville, UT 84104
(801) 451-9779
www.karenfosterdesign.com
Paper Punches

Krylon Products
101 N. Prospect Avenue
Cleveland, OH 44115
(800) 797-3332
www.krylon.com
Spray Adhesive

Loew-Cornell
563 Chestnut Avenue
Teaneck, NJ 07666
(201) 836-7070
www.loewcornell.com
Brushes

McGill Incorporated
131 E. Prairie Street
Marengo, IL 60512
(800) 982-9884
www.mcgillinc.com
Paper Punches

The Paper Patch
(800) 397-2737
www.paperpatch.com
Scrapbook Papers

Plaid Enterprises, Inc.
P.O. Box 7600
Norcross, GA 30091
(800) 842-4197
www.plaidonline.com
Mod Podge

Therm O Web
770 Glenn Avenue
Wheeling, IL 60090
(847) 520-5200
www.thermoweb.com
HeatnBond Lite Iron on Adhesive
PeelnStick (Double-sided adhesive sheet and tape)

Walnut Hollow
1409 State Road 23
Dodgeville, WI 53533
(800) 950-5101
www.walnuthollow.com
Wooden Arch Clock-Medium (53202)
Clock Components
Mail Box

Index

Let your imagination soar with these other titles from North Light Books!

These and other fine imprint books are available at your local art & craft retailer, bookstore, online supplier or by calling 1-800-448-0915.

Bright Ideas in Papercrafts

Bring a personal touch to every celebration, holiday and special occasion. Bright Ideas in Papercrafts gives guidelines and advice for creating 23 elegant projects using all of your favorite tools, from decorative edging scissors to paper crimpers, archival papers and more. It's easy, fun and fast! Start creating hand-crafted keepsakes that will be treasured for years to come.
ISBN 1-58180-352-4, paperback, 128 pages, #32325-K

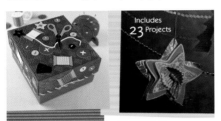

Collage Creations

Collage Creations is the perfect introduction to the exciting world of collage. In this guide, readers will learn how to use a variety of easy collage techniques to make ordinary items extraordinary and fill their home with their own, personalized artwork. Featuring over 20 step-by-step projects and a section on stress-free design, this book will inspire you to create collages on frames, boxes, journals, tabletops and more!
ISBN 1-58180-546-2, paperback, 128 pages, #32894-K

Whimsical Accents for Your Home

Paint something irresistible for your home with Whimsical Accents for Your Home. Inside you'll be able to make 25 whimsical home décor projects that are fun and easy, even if you've never lifted a paintbrush. With simple paint effects and pre-cut wooden embellishments you'll create projects including a frame with cut-out letters, a funky floral lamp, sophisticated candle holders and a garden vegetables bin.
ISBN 1-58180-590-X, paperback, 64 pages, #33061-K

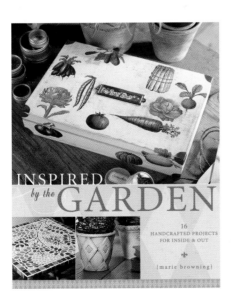

Inspired by the Garden

Inspired by the Garden presents 12 garden-inspired projects for inside and out. Using a range of crafting techniques and materials, this book showcases fun yet sophisticated garden decor projects perfect for crafters of all skill levels. Featuring popular garden motifs, projects include mosaic garden tables, matching pots and watering can, a garden apron and more!
ISBN 1-58180-434-2, paperback, 128 pages, #32630-K